ADHD Organization and Cleaning 5-in-1

Get Organized and Stay Consistent with Easy Routines and Systems for Organizing and Keeping Your Home and Life Clean

Vivian Whitmore

Claim Your Free Bonus

As a thank you for reading, I've put together a powerful digital bonus pack to help you apply what you've learned — even if you only have a few minutes a day.

 Inside you'll find:

✔ Quick-access emotional reset tools
✔ A printable clarity map for focus and purpose
✔ 30 powerful journaling prompts
✔ Daily progress & reflection trackers
✔ A mini affirmation deck for calm and confidence

Access below to download your full bonus pack:

https://livetolearn.lpages.co/vivian-withmore-adhd-organization-and-cleaning-5-in-1-paperback/

Or, scan the QR code

ADHD Organization and Cleaning 5-in-1: Get Organized and Stay Consistent with Easy Routines and Systems for Organizing and Keeping Your Home and Life Clean

As a psychologist, I found *ADHD Organization and Cleaning 5-in-1: Get Organized and Stay Consistent with Easy Routines and Systems for Organizing and Keeping Your Home and Life Clean* by Vivian Whitmore to be both practical and deeply validating for individuals with ADHD. This excellent resource bridges neuroscience, behavioral strategies, and compassionate guidance, making it an invaluable tool for anyone struggling to create order in their environment and their mind.

The opening chapters on routines, habits, and the effects of clutter establish a realistic framework. Rather than framing clutter as moral failure, the author presents it as an executive functioning challenge that can be resolved by being broken down into achievable steps. This approach aligns with cognitive-behavioral strategies I have recommended in therapy—reducing shame and highlighting personal strengths and skill-building.

I particularly appreciated the chapter on how progress beats perfection, which reframes productivity as a continuum. ADHD brains are prone to all-or-nothing thinking, so emphasizing incremental improvement is not only motivational, but also protective against discouragement.

ADHD Organization and Cleaning 5-in-1: Get Organized and Stay Consistent with Easy Routines and Systems for Organizing and Keeping Your Home and Life Clean provides several strategies that are effective in aiding people with ADHD in achieving a more organized and structured daily life. For instance, the 10-minute tidy illustrates this beautifully in the first chapter. It is a time-limited task that generates momentum and provides a "small win," which in turn reinforces positive behavior.

The sections on energy mapping and environmental anchors demonstrate psychological insight into how context shapes behavior. By aligning tasks with natural energy peaks and using visual cues in the environment, the book harnesses principles of behavioral psychology in a way that is accessible and actionable.

From a clinical perspective, I was also impressed by the exploration of routines, habits, and time management. The discussion of time blocking and seasonal routines shows sensitivity to the cyclical patterns many clients with ADHD experience. The inclusion of a cleaning toolkit provides a concrete, sensory-friendly entry point to tasks that often feel abstract or overwhelming.

ADHD Organization and Cleaning 5-in-1: Get Organized and Stay Consistent with Easy Routines and Systems for Organizing and Keeping Your Home and Life Clean does not shy away from the emotional dimension of organization. The chapters on why a clean space calms the brain and on bouncing back after setbacks underscore the role of environment in emotional regulation. These insights mirror research showing that reduced visual clutter can lower cognitive load and support attentional control.

As a psychologist, I value the inclusion of reflection questions and quizzes, as these tools transform the book from a passive guide into an interactive self-help tool. This promotes metacognition—a key therapeutic goal in ADHD management—by encouraging readers to notice patterns, strengths, and areas of growth.

ADHD Organization and Cleaning 5-in-1: Get Organized and Stay Consistent with Easy Routines and Systems for Organizing and Keeping Your Home and Life Clean is both scientifically informed and practically grounded. I am confident that it will offer readers with ADHD—and those supporting them—an empowering roadmap for creating environments that foster focus, calm, and sustainable routines. I will be recommending it in my clinical practice.

Carolina Estevez, Psy.D.

Licensed Psychologist

TABLE OF CONTENTS

INTRODUCTION:

WELCOME TO YOUR ORGANIZED LIFE

The idea of "getting organized" can feel like a mountain to climb, especially for those of us with an ADHD brain. The world often seems built for neurotypical minds, a place where to-do lists are linear, focus is constant, and "just do it" is considered helpful advice. Let's be honest: that's not our reality. The well-intentioned advice of "just make a list" or "stick to a schedule" often rings hollow, creating a cycle of aspiration, frustration, and eventual shame. We know what we "should" do, but the bridge between intention and action can feel impossible to cross. This persistent friction, the energy spent trying to force ourselves into a system that simply doesn't fit, is a silent but exhausting tax on our mental and emotional well-being.

This book is a guide for a different kind of reality. It's not about forcing yourself into a system that doesn't fit; it's about building one that does. It's for the person who starts cleaning the kitchen and ends up organizing the entire garage because **hyperfocus** takes over. It's for the person who feels overwhelmed by a single messy drawer and a person who can't find their keys for the tenth time this week. It's for you. This is an invitation to stop fighting your brain and start working with it. Instead of trying to become someone you're not, we will focus on designing a life that celebrates who you are.

This is a 5-in-1 guide that focuses on tangible, flexible, and sustainable strategies. You won't find any one-size-fits-all solutions here, because your brain is unique. Instead, you'll find a **toolkit** of concepts and systems that you can adapt to your life, your home, and your unique way of thinking. We'll show you how to work with your brain's natural tendencies, like harnessing hyperfocus for deep cleaning, rather than constantly fighting against them. This is not a journey to a perfectly sterile, minimalist space; it's a journey to a peaceful, functional home that supports your passions and allows you to thrive.

Understanding the "ADHD Tax"

Before we can build a new system, we must first acknowledge the one we've been living with: the **"ADHD Tax."** This is the mental, emotional, and even financial cost of living with executive dysfunction in a world that doesn't account for it. It's the anxiety of a late bill, the shame of a messy house when guests are coming over, the frustration of a project that never gets finished, and the lost time spent searching for misplaced items. It's the constant, low-level stress that comes from feeling like you're always playing catch-up.

This volume is designed to help you start recouping that tax. We will do this not by forcing you into a rigid mold, but by building **external systems** that compensate for your internal challenges. Our goal is to reduce the friction in your daily life, freeing up your mental energy for what truly matters. We'll show you how a simple routine can save you hours of anxiety and how a small reward can be the difference between a task being done or remaining abandoned indefinitely.

The 5 Pillars of Your New Toolkit

This book is divided into five core sections, each a pillar of your new organizational toolkit. They are designed to be read in order, as each concept builds upon the last.

- **Pillar 1: The Foundations of a Flexible Routine.** We'll begin by challenging the very idea of a "perfect" routine. You'll learn to redefine your relationship with clutter, embrace the **"good enough" mindset**, and harness the **power of small wins**. This is a chapter about unlearning old, shaming habits and embracing a compassionate, realistic perspective. We will lay the groundwork for a routine that works *with* your fluctuating energy levels, not against them.

- **Pillar 2: Mastering Routines and Habit Formation.** With the right mindset in place, we'll dive into the practical application of building routines. You'll learn how to implement a **Morning Reset** to start your day with intention, an **Evening Routine** to calm your mind and prepare for the next day, and a **Weekend Deep Dive** that transforms overwhelming tasks into manageable projects. We'll use concepts like **micro-habits** and **habit stacking** to build these routines with minimal effort.

- **Pillar 3: Decluttering and Organizing Made Easy.** Decluttering can feel like an impossible task, but it doesn't have to be. We'll introduce you to a simple, guilt-free method for getting started. You'll learn to identify and conquer your personal **"chaos hotspots,"** using the **"Keep, Toss, Donate"** method to make swift, confident decisions. This chapter is about creating a functional, peaceful home without having to get rid of everything you own.

- **Pillar 4: The Cleaning Toolkit and Time Management.** We'll shift our focus from organizing to cleaning, but with a twist. You'll learn how to build a simple, effective **"cleaning toolkit"** that is always at the ready. We'll also explore **time-management hacks** and **gamification techniques** like the **"Beat the Clock"** method that turn tedious chores into fun, engaging challenges. This is about making chores less of a burden and more of a game you can win.

- **Pillar 5: Staying Consistent and Bouncing Back.** This is the most critical chapter of the book. Consistency is the ultimate goal, but for the ADHD brain, it can feel impossible. You'll learn the **"Don't Break the Chain"** method to build momentum and the **"Art of the Rebound"** to get back on track without judgment. This chapter is about building a system that is resilient enough to handle the inevitable moments when life gets in the way.

A Note on Neurodiversity

Neurodiversity is the idea that differences in brain function are just that, differences, and not deficits. Your ADHD brain is a powerful engine with incredible potential. It is creative, energetic, empathetic, and often capable of intense, focused problem-solving. This book isn't about "fixing" your ADHD; it's about empowering you to navigate life's challenges with confidence and **self-compassion**. The strategies you'll find here are designed to work for you, not against you. They are about creating a sense of peace and control without sacrificing who you are.

We will not talk about your brain as being "broken." Instead, we will talk about its unique wiring and how to build a life that is perfectly suited to it. Think of your ADHD brain not as a faulty machine, but as a high-performance sports car with a unique set of controls. You wouldn't try to drive a sports car like a family sedan. Similarly, you shouldn't try to force your brain into a neurotypical mold. This book will give you the manual for that sports car—the tools and the understanding to drive it with skill and confidence.

The Power of Self-Compassion

This entire book is built on a foundation of **self-compassion**. We will not talk about "shoulds" or "failures." We will talk about **learning opportunities** and **systems that don't fit**. The voice in your head that tells you you're not good enough is a powerful enemy of progress. The most important tool you will learn is how to silence that voice with kindness.

Self-compassion is not an excuse for inaction; it is the engine for sustainable change. When you fall off the wagon, self-compassion is the voice that says, "It's okay, let's try again tomorrow," instead of "You've ruined everything." This single shift in perspective is often the difference between a temporary slip-up and a permanent derailment. It is the core principle that will allow you to build a life that is not just organized, but also forgiving and kind.

To All Readers

While this book is titled "ADHD Organization and Cleaning 5-in-1," the principles and strategies within are valuable for anyone seeking to bring more order and calm into their life. The challenges of motivation, task initiation, and maintaining routines are universal human experiences, even if they are more pronounced for those with ADHD.

- **For the student** struggling to manage their assignments and keep their dorm room tidy.
- **For the professional** who feels overwhelmed by a mountain of emails and a cluttered desk.
- **For the parent** who wants to create a more peaceful home for their family.

This book is for you. Inclusivity is at the heart of this book, and the goal is to provide a guide that is welcoming and helpful to all. The strategies are designed to be accessible and low-friction, because we believe that the best systems are the ones that are easy to use.

So, let's begin this journey. Let's redefine what it means to be organized, and create a space and a life that truly works for you. This isn't a race to the finish line; it's a marathon of small, intentional steps. Your organized future is not a destination to be reached, but a life to be lived. And it begins right now.

BOOK ONE:

THE FOUNDATIONS OF A FLEXIBLE ROUTINE

CHAPTER 1:

FROM OVERWHELMED TO EMPOWERED: REDEFINING YOUR RELATIONSHIP WITH CLUTTER SO IT NO LONGER CONTROLS YOU.

For many with ADHD, clutter isn't just a mess; it's a source of shame, anxiety, and overwhelm. We look at a disorganized space and see a reflection of our own perceived failures. The endless piles of clothes, the stacks of mail, the overflowing countertops—each item feels like a judgment. The constant visual noise creates a persistent cognitive burden, much like having a dozen browser tabs open in your mind at all times. It's an energy drain that makes it harder to focus, think clearly, and feel at peace in your own home.

What if we could change that narrative? This chapter is about shifting your perspective. Instead of viewing clutter as a moral failing, let's see it as a puzzle to be solved. Let's redefine our relationship with our things and our space.

The Problem with "Getting Rid of Everything"

Conventional wisdom often suggests ruthless decluttering, throwing out everything that doesn't "spark joy" or serve an immediate purpose. For the ADHD brain, this can be a recipe for disaster. **Decision fatigue** is a real and powerful force. Faced with a mountain of choices about what to keep and what to discard, many of us become paralyzed and abandon the task entirely. The result? The clutter remains, and the feeling of failure intensifies. For a brain that already struggles with executive functions like prioritization and sustained attention, a task that demands hundreds of micro-decisions is a system designed to fail.

The first step isn't to get rid of things; it's to understand them. What purpose do these items serve, even if they're not in their "right" place? The stack of books on your nightstand might be a reminder of your passion for reading. The pile of mail could be a sign that you're an active, engaged person with a lot going on. Acknowledging this can lessen the shame and allow you to approach the task with a clearer mind. The goal is to move past the judgment and see the objects for what they are.

The Power of Small Shifts

Instead of a complete overhaul, we'll start with small, manageable shifts. The goal is to move from being overwhelmed by your space to feeling in control of it. We'll introduce a new vocabulary and a new mindset.

- **From "Mess" to "Opportunity":** Every cluttered surface is an opportunity to create a system that works for you. Instead of a daunting mountain, you see a series of small, solvable problems.
- **From "Should" to "Could":** Instead of "I *should* clean this room," try "I *could* spend ten minutes on this one corner." This simple word change lowers the pressure and makes the task feel optional, which can make it easier to start.

- **From "All at Once" to "One at a Time":** Focus on a single item, a single drawer, or a single surface. This breaks the cycle of overwhelm and allows you to build momentum. This is the core of **micro-decluttering**, a powerful technique that delivers a quick win and a small dose of dopamine, encouraging you to continue.

By redefining your relationship with clutter, you're healing your mindset. You're acknowledging that your brain works differently, and that's okay. You're giving yourself permission to find a new, more compassionate way forward. You are taking back control, one small shift at a time.

CHAPTER 2:

THE MYTH OF "NORMAL" & THE POWER OF "ENOUGH": HOW PROGRESS BEATS PERFECTION EVERY TIME.

Often, we see perfectly curated homes on social media and feel like we're falling short. This pressure to be "normal" or "perfect" can be crushing for someone with ADHD. It often leads to a cycle of trying to meet unrealistic expectations, burning out, and then feeling even worse about ourselves.

This chapter is a permission slip to embrace imperfection. It's about letting go of the myth of normal and finding the power in "enough." The constant pressure to meet an impossible standard of "normal" is a self-defeating game. "Normal" for a neurotypical person might involve a structured, linear approach to tasks, but for the ADHD brain, that path is often a source of frustration, not success. By shedding the expectation of conforming to a norm that doesn't fit, you can begin to build a system that works with your brain, not against it.

Progress Over Perfection

The idea of "**progress over perfection**" is a cornerstone of a flexible routine. For the ADHD brain, perfectionism is often a form of procrastination. We often don't start a task because we're afraid we can't do it perfectly, so we don't do it at all. The goal isn't to have a spotless, show-ready home every single day. The goal is to make small, consistent improvements that make your life easier and less stressful. This is about embracing the messy, incremental nature of real life.

Think of it like a game: you're not aiming for a perfect score on the first try. You're simply trying to get to the next level. This mindset shift is crucial. It gives you permission to make mistakes, to have a bad day, and to keep going anyway. It's the difference between seeing a day without cleaning as a total failure and seeing it as a temporary pause.

Here are a few examples of what "good enough" looks like in practice:

- **A "Good Enough" Kitchen:** Your kitchen doesn't have to look like a magazine cover. If the counters are clear enough to prepare a meal and the dishes are done enough to not attract pests, that's a win.
- **A "Functional" Closet:** Instead of a color-coded, perfectly folded closet, aim for one where you can find what you need without a search party.
- **A "Manageable" Routine:** A routine that you can stick to 80% of the time is far more valuable than a "perfect" routine you abandon after a week.

This approach acknowledges that life is dynamic and that a rigid routine will inevitably fail. A flexible routine, however, can bend without breaking.

The Power of "Enough"

Knowing what "**enough**" looks like is a superpower for the ADHD brain. It prevents the all-or-nothing thinking that often derails our efforts. When you can define what "enough" means for a specific task, you can complete it and move on without the pressure of having to make it flawless. This is a powerful tool against the "I'll just do it all later" mentality. It provides a clear finish line, which is essential for a brain that struggles with sustaining attention on a single task.

For example, "enough" might mean:

- Doing laundry is "enough" when you have clean clothes to wear for the week, not when every last sock is folded and put away.
- A clean living room is "enough" when the floor is clear of obstacles and you have a comfortable place to sit, not when the couch cushions are perfectly fluffed.

This chapter is about giving yourself grace. Your brain is wired for creativity, quick thinking, and dynamic problem-solving. It's not wired for the monotonous, rigid systems that society often promotes. By embracing "enough," you're not lowering your standards—you're setting **realistic ones that allow you to thrive**.

This is not a license to give up; it's a license to succeed on your own terms. It's a fundamental shift from a mindset of self-criticism to one of self-compassion. The goal is to create a peaceful, functional life, not a perfectly staged one. This approach honors your unique strengths and acknowledges your challenges without judgment. When you can let go of the pressure to be "normal," you can start living a life that is authentically yours. You are enough, and so is your effort.

CHAPTER 3:

THE 10-MINUTE TIDY: SMALL, ADHD-FRIENDLY WINS THAT CREATE BIG MOMENTUM.

The greatest enemy of an organized life is **overwhelm**. When a task seems too big, our brains tend to shut down, and we do nothing at all. This phenomenon is particularly acute for the ADHD brain, which struggles with task initiation and prioritization. A large, unstructured task like "clean the living room" is a perfect trigger for analysis paralysis. The key to breaking this cycle is to start small. This chapter is dedicated to the power of tiny, achievable actions that build momentum and make a noticeable difference without triggering decision fatigue.

The 10-Minute Tidy

This is a simple, yet profoundly effective, strategy. The goal is to bypass the internal debate and just start. Set a timer for 10 minutes and focus on a single, small area. The rules are simple and designed to remove mental roadblocks:

- **Don't plan; just start.** Pick a surface (a countertop, a coffee table, a section of the floor) and begin putting things away. The act of starting, even without a perfect plan, is the most critical step.

- **Focus on "home."** Put items where they belong. If an item doesn't have a home, don't worry about it for now. Just put it in a temporary "to-sort" bin. This single rule prevents you from getting bogged down in the minutiae of where to store something, allowing you to maintain focus on the task at hand.

- **Stop when the timer goes off.** When the ten minutes are up, you're done. No matter how much you've accomplished, you can walk away with a win. The hard stop provides a sense of closure and prevents a 10-minute tidy from spiraling into an exhaustive, multi-hour ordeal.

The genius of this method is that it bypasses the planning phase, which is often a major roadblock for the ADHD brain. The difficulty with the planning phase of a task for those with ADHD is rooted in the brain's executive functions. The prefrontal cortex (PFC), the part of the brain responsible for these functions, is crucial for skills like:

- **Task initiation:** The ability to start a task.
- **Planning and prioritization:** Breaking down a large task into manageable steps and deciding which to do first.
- **Working memory:** Holding and manipulating information in your mind.

In the ADHD brain, there is a **dysregulation of dopamine and norepinephrine** in the PFC. These neurotransmitters are essential for communication between brain cells and are directly involved in motivation, reward, and attention. When a task requires significant planning, the PFC needs a lot of dopamine to function effectively. A large, unstructured task like "clean the living room" demands a high level of executive function, but the ADHD brain struggles to produce the necessary dopamine to activate this process. This results in **analysis paralysis**—a state where the brain is overwhelmed by the number of steps required and never sends the signal to start.

How the Method Works

The "10-minute tidy" works because it circumvents this neurobiological roadblock. Instead of relying on a high-demand planning process, it turns the task into a low-demand, immediate action.

1. **Reduces Cognitive Load:** By setting a short timer and focusing on a single, small area, the method dramatically reduces the cognitive load on the PFC. The brain doesn't have to plan a whole-room cleaning; it just has to focus on one simple instruction: "tidy for 10 minutes."

2. **Triggers Action, Not Planning:** The simplicity of the instruction moves the task from the realm of complex executive function to the realm of simple habit formation. The act of setting a timer serves as a powerful external cue that overrides the internal struggle to initiate.

3. **Provides an Immediate Reward:** The quick, visible progress made in just 10 minutes provides a fast dopamine hit, which is a powerful motivator for the ADHD brain. This positive feedback loop makes it much easier to start the task again next time, slowly building a new, more effective neural pathway.

In short, the method doesn't try to "fix" the brain's challenges with planning; it simply finds a brilliant way to go around them.

Other Small Wins

The 10-minute tidy is just one example. There are countless other small, manageable steps you can integrate into your day to build a habit of proactive organization:

- **The "One-Thing" Rule:** Before leaving a room, find one thing to put away. It can be a mug, a book, a stray sock. Just one thing. This is a subtle yet powerful trick that turns a mindless transition into a moment of intentionality, preventing small messes from accumulating into large ones.

- **The "Micro-Clean":** While waiting for your coffee to brew or a pot to boil, wipe down a small section of the counter. These short, otherwise "dead" moments in your day can be repurposed for a small, productive task.

- **The "Two-Minute Rule":** If a task takes less than two minutes to complete, do it immediately. This could be putting a dish in the dishwasher, responding to a quick email, or taking out a small bag of trash. This rule is a direct counter to procrastination, as it leverages the principle that it takes more mental energy to put off a small task than it does to simply do it.

- **The "Landing Strip Reset":** Before bed, take just two minutes to clear your main "landing strip", the entry table, kitchen counter, or coffee table where things tend to pile up. This ensures you wake up to a clear, calm space, which sets a positive tone for the entire day.

These small wins may seem insignificant on their own, but their cumulative effect is profound. They build confidence, establish new neural pathways, and, most importantly, show you that you are capable of creating order in your life. By celebrating these small victories, you're retraining your brain to associate cleaning and organizing with a sense of accomplishment, not with dread or overwhelm.

CHAPTER 4:

WHY A CLEAN SPACE CALMS YOUR BRAIN: THE NEURO-PSYCHOLOGY BEHIND YOUR ENVIRONMENT AND FOCUS.

Our brains are constantly processing information from our environment. For the ADHD brain, this can be an overwhelming flood of sensory input. A cluttered space isn't just visually unappealing; it's a **cognitive drain**. This chapter explores the psychological link between your physical environment and your mental state, revealing how a cleaner, more organized space can lead to a calmer, more focused mind.

The Cognitive Load of Clutter

Every object in your field of vision demands a tiny amount of your brain's attention. A stack of papers on a table, a pile of clothes on a chair, a jumble of items on a counter, each is a silent distraction. For a brain that already struggles with filtering out irrelevant stimuli, this creates a significant cognitive load. The prefrontal cortex (PFC), the brain's executive control center, is responsible for tasks like filtering out distractions and sustaining attention. Research shows that in the ADHD brain, the PFC can have reduced activity and dysregulation of key neurotransmitters, making this filtering process much more difficult.

A cluttered environment essentially bombards the brain with a constant stream of visual data that it cannot easily ignore. It's like a computer with dozens of unnecessary programs running in the background, consuming valuable processing power. This persistent visual noise forces the brain to constantly make micro-decisions: "What is that item? Where should it be? Do I need to deal with it?" This perpetual state of low-grade mental effort leads to **decision fatigue** and, eventually, a feeling of being completely overwhelmed. A clean and organized space, by contrast, reduces this cognitive load. It provides a sense of visual calm, allowing your brain to allocate its limited resources to what's truly important. It's not about an empty room, but about creating a functional, peaceful environment where your mind can finally rest and focus.

The Link Between Order and Emotion

The connection between your physical surroundings and your emotional state is a well-documented psychological phenomenon. For the ADHD brain, a tidy space can have a direct and positive impact on your emotions and motivation. The act of cleaning or organizing, even in small doses, can be a powerful form of mindfulness. It grounds you in the present moment and gives you a tangible sense of control over your immediate surroundings. This feeling of control is particularly important for people with ADHD who often feel a lack of control over their thoughts, impulses, and routines.

Furthermore, a messy environment is a potent source of stress. Studies have shown a correlation between high levels of household clutter and elevated **cortisol** levels, the body's primary stress hormone. A cluttered space is a constant, physical reminder of uncompleted tasks and disorganized thoughts, which can trigger a continuous, low-grade stress response.

The Brain's Need for a Predictive Environment

Beyond just visual clutter, the brain's need for order is deeply tied to its desire for predictability. The lack of a dedicated "home" for an object creates a constant need for the brain to categorize and remember where things are. This is another significant source of cognitive load. An organized space is one that is predictable; every item has a place, and you don't have to expend mental energy searching for your keys or wallet. This predictability frees up your working memory for creative thought and problem-solving. It also reduces "future anxiety", the dread of a task you know you have to do but haven't started.

CHAPTER 5:

SYSTEMS BUILT FOR YOU: CREATING A CUSTOM APPROACH THAT WORKS WITH YOUR BRAIN, NOT AGAINST IT.

Traditional organization advice often fails the ADHD community because it's built on a foundation of rigid rules and systems that demand a level of sustained focus and routine that many of us simply don't have. This final chapter of Book 1 is about rejecting that rigid rulebook and empowering you to build a custom-built system that works with your unique brain.

From "Should" to "What If?"

Instead of asking, "What should a clean home look like?" start asking, "What if I organized my life in a way that feels natural to me?" This is about experimenting and finding what works.

- What if I didn't fold my clothes perfectly, but instead created a simple "toss and go" system for my drawers?
- What if I didn't file every piece of paper, but instead created a single "action" box for everything that needs my attention?
- What if my daily routine isn't the same every day, but instead I have a flexible set of micro-habits that I can adapt to my energy levels?

Custom-Building Your Tools

Your organizational system should be a reflection of you, not a reflection of a Pinterest board. Think about what your brain needs to function well.

- **Out of Sight, Out of Mind? Or Out of Mind, Out of Sight?** Some people with ADHD need to have things out where they can see them. For others, visual clutter is a huge distraction. Figure out which one you are and design your storage accordingly.
- **Use Visual Cues:** Use clear containers, labels with pictures, and open shelving to make it easy for your brain to see where things belong.
- **Embrace Your Strengths:** Use your hyperfocus to do a deep-clean on a specific day of the month. Use your creativity to come up with new, fun ways to organize.

CHAPTER 6:

ENERGY MAPPING: ORGANIZING AROUND YOUR NATURAL RHYTHMS

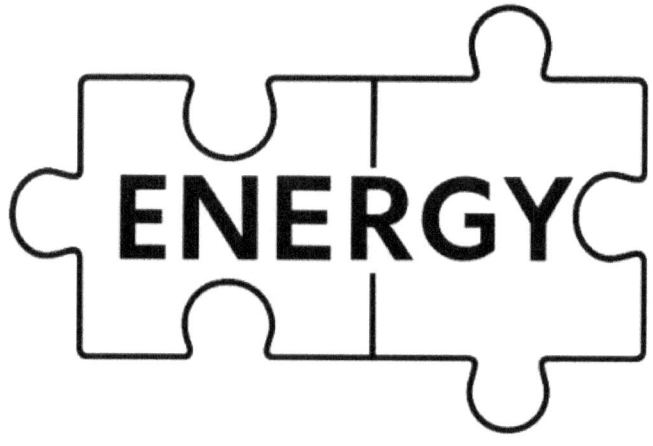

The ADHD Energy Puzzle

If you live with ADHD, you already know this: your energy levels don't run in neat, predictable lines. Some days, you wake up brimming with enthusiasm and dive headfirst into projects you've been putting off for months. Other days, even brushing your teeth feels like scaling a mountain. This inconsistency is not laziness or lack of discipline, it's neurobiology. The ADHD brain processes dopamine differently, which affects not only focus but also motivation and energy regulation.

Understanding your unique energy rhythms is like finding a secret map of your brain. Instead of pushing against your dips or wasting your peaks, you can align your tasks with your natural flow. That's what **energy mapping** is about: noticing when you're sharp, sluggish, restless, or calm, and using that awareness to work *with* your brain, not against it.

Why Energy Matters More Than Time

Most productivity systems tell you to "manage your time." For ADHD, time is slippery. You may intend to clean for "just 15 minutes" but suddenly two hours have vanished, or you may underestimate a task so much that it snowballs into overwhelm.

But energy? Energy is tangible. You *feel* it. You know the difference between the morning when your brain is buzzing with ideas versus the afternoon crash where you can't remember what you walked into the room for.

Managing energy instead of time is a game-changer because:

- **Energy is the fuel**: If the tank is empty, no amount of scheduling will move you forward.
- **Energy impacts focus**: Higher energy often means better executive functioning.
- **Energy determines sustainability**: Matching tasks to your natural rhythm reduces burnout.

By learning to observe your patterns, you stop asking, *"What should I be doing at 3 PM?"* and start asking, *"What kind of energy do I have right now, and what tasks fit that?"*

Step 1: Discover Your Energy Peaks and Valleys

Energy mapping starts with awareness. For one week, try this simple exercise:

1. **Create an "Energy Journal".** Divide the day into blocks (morning, mid-morning, afternoon, evening, night).
2. **Rate your energy.** Use a simple 1–5 scale (1 = drained, 5 = high-energy).
3. **Notice the patterns.** Are mornings clear but afternoons foggy? Do you get a second wind at night?

Over time, you'll see trends. Maybe you consistently struggle with focus after lunch but come alive around 7 PM. Or maybe your best mental clarity is in the early morning before distractions pile up.

This awareness alone can transform your routines. Instead of forcing yourself into "morning productivity" because everyone says it's best, you learn to design your schedule around *your* truth.

Step 2: Assign "Energy-Friendly" Tasks

Once you've mapped your rhythms, match them with the right type of tasks. Think of your energy like a spectrum:

- **High-Energy / High-Focus Times:**
    - Decluttering sessions
    - Paying bills or handling paperwork
    - Tackling chaos hotspots (kitchen, closet, garage)
    - Deep-cleaning tasks that require sustained attention
- **Medium-Energy / Moderate-Focus Times:**
    - Tidying (10-minute resets)
    - Folding laundry
    - Prepping meals
    - Doing "batch tasks" like responding to emails
- **Low-Energy / Low-Focus Times:**
    - Brain dumps
    - Listening to podcasts while wiping counters
    - Sorting small items into bins
    - Reflection or light planning for the next day

The point isn't to always be productive, it's to **choose wisely**. If you try to do your taxes during a low-energy crash, you'll get stuck and feel frustrated. But if you pair that same slump with a mindless task like folding towels, you'll keep momentum without burning out.

Step 3: Build "Energy Anchors"

Energy naturally fluctuates, but you can create anchors that help stabilize your flow:

- **Hydration & Snacks:** The ADHD brain is extra sensitive to dips in blood sugar. Keep protein-rich snacks nearby.

- **Movement Breaks:** Physical activity boosts dopamine and norepinephrine, both critical for focus. A 5-minute walk can reset a slump.
- **Sensory Cues:** Music, scents (peppermint or citrus), or even lighting changes can refresh your energy.
- **Mini Routines:** Rituals like the "5-Minute Reset" after lunch can act as anchors, signaling your brain it's time to shift gears.

These don't eliminate energy dips, but they soften the crash and give you reliable tools to re-engage.

Step 4: Respect the ADHD "Second Wind"

Many with ADHD experience bursts of energy late at night, what some call the "ADHD second wind". While the world says you should be winding down, your brain suddenly wants to reorganize the bookshelf or deep-clean the fridge.

Instead of fighting this, learn to channel it responsibly:

- Use it for **quiet tasks** (organizing digital files, folding laundry, prepping for tomorrow).
- Protect your sleep by setting a **wind-down timer**, an alarm that signals "wrap up in 20 minutes."
- Keep a "night box" or tray: a place where you can toss items you want to handle tomorrow instead of spiraling into a midnight project.

This honors your rhythm without letting it sabotage your rest.

Step 5: Plan with "Flexible Blocks"

Forget rigid hour-by-hour scheduling. Use flexible blocks based on energy:

- **Morning Boost Block (High Energy):** Big projects, paperwork, creative work.
- **Afternoon Slump Block (Low/Medium Energy):** Tidying, chores, low-brain tasks.
- **Evening Reset Block (Medium Energy):** Launchpad prep, quick cleanup, self-care.

- **Late-Night Burst Block (Optional High Energy):** Quiet, contained projects.

By labeling blocks by energy instead of time, you give yourself grace and freedom. If your "boost" shows up later than expected, you can shift tasks accordingly without guilt.

ADHD-Friendly Hacks for Energy Management

1. **Use Visual Energy Trackers:** Color-coded stickers or charts to mark high/low energy times each day.

2. **Task-Swap Lists:** Keep two lists—"high-focus" tasks and "low-focus" tasks. Choose based on your current state.

3. **Pair Energy with Rewards:** After using a peak to tackle something hard, reward yourself immediately (snack, 5 minutes scrolling, or a victory dance).

4. **Micro-Rest Stations:** Set up cozy nooks with blankets, water, and low-stim activities so recovery doesn't become avoidance.

Common Pitfalls (and Fixes)

- **Pitfall:** "I planned to do paperwork in my high-energy block, but I wasted it scrolling."
  - **Fix:** Remove distractions in advance; pair paperwork with a motivating playlist or co-working session.
- **Pitfall:** "I get frustrated when my energy map doesn't match every day."
  - **Fix:** Remember, it's a *map*, not a guarantee. Energy shifts with sleep, stress, and hormones. The goal is awareness, not control.
- **Pitfall:** "I try to force big tasks into my low-energy slumps."
  - **Fix:** Redefine "success." Use slumps for resets, brain dumps, or light chores instead of expecting peak performance.

Real-Life Example: Emily's Laundry Dilemma

Emily dreaded laundry. By the time she faced the overflowing basket, she was always in her 3 PM slump. She'd start folding, lose steam, and leave half-finished piles everywhere.

Through energy mapping, she discovered her **highest energy was 9–11 AM**. So instead of saving laundry for later, she made it her **morning focus task** twice a week. By pairing folding with an upbeat playlist, she finished loads with ease. For her **slump block**, she reassigned easier tasks like matching socks or putting folded clothes away.

The result? A routine that fit her rhythms, not one that fought against them.

CHAPTER 7:

ENVIRONMENTAL ANCHORS:
DESIGNING SPACES THAT CUE ACTION

Why Your Environment Matters More Than You Think

Living with ADHD often feels like you're carrying your to-do list in your head ... but the list has holes in it, and items keep falling out. You intend to take out the recycling, but by the time you pass the kitchen bin, your brain has already jumped to something else. You want to clean your desk, but your mind gets hijacked by the pile of unopened mail.

The truth is, your environment is a *partner*. Every object around you sends a message, consciously or unconsciously. The trick is to design your spaces so they **cue the behaviors you want** instead of constantly derailing you. This is what I call **environmental anchors**: intentional, visible, and supportive cues in your space that make routines easier to start and habits easier to keep.

The Science of Environmental Cues

ADHD brains struggle with working memory and self-directed recall. In plain language: "out of sight, out of mind" is brutally real. If something isn't right in front of you, it might as well not exist. That's why bills get forgotten once tucked in a drawer, why half-finished laundry sits in the machine until it smells, and why a planner buried in your bag never gets used.

Research on habit formation shows that **environmental design** often has a bigger impact than willpower. Psychologist Kurt Lewin described behavior as a function of both the person *and* the environment. Change the environment, and the behavior often follows.

For ADHD, this means we need to make **the desired action the easiest, most obvious choice**, and remove friction for starting. Environmental anchors reduce the reliance on memory and motivation and instead use **visual and physical prompts** to guide behavior.

Step 1: Identify Your "Forgetting Zones"

Before you start adding anchors, notice where your environment is currently *working against you*. Ask yourself:

- Where do I often forget steps in routines?
- Which spaces feel overwhelming or chaotic?
- Where does clutter pile up, no matter how often I tidy?
- What do I avoid doing because it feels too far away, too hidden, or too complicated?

These are the prime spots for anchors. For example:

- If shoes pile by the door, maybe your current shoe storage is too hidden or inconvenient.
- If you constantly forget to take vitamins, maybe they're stuck in a closed cupboard.
- If mail stacks up unopened, maybe you don't have a landing spot for it.

Awareness is the first step to creating better support.

Step 2: Make the Invisible Visible

ADHD-friendly environments thrive on **visibility**. When you can see it, you remember it. When you hide it, it disappears.

Examples of visibility anchors:

- Clear bins instead of opaque boxes.
- Hooks instead of drawers (for keys, bags, coats).
- Open shelving for frequently used items.
- Labels, even if obvious, so your brain doesn't have to think.

Think of visibility as removing the mental step of recall. Instead of your brain needing to remember *"where did I put my scissors?"*, the scissors live in a jar on your desk, easy to spot.

Step 3: Create "Behavior Triggers"

The most powerful anchors are ones that directly cue the action you want.

- **Water Cue:** Keep a water bottle on your desk to trigger hydration.
- **Launchpad Cue:** Place your packed bag, shoes, and keys by the door so leaving the house feels automatic.
- **Cleaning Cue:** Store wipes in every room so a quick counter swipe doesn't require a trip to the supply closet.
- **Bedtime Cue:** Place your book and lamp within arm's reach to make reading instead of scrolling the default.

These are not just convenience hacks. They're **friction removers**, each anchor lowers the effort needed to start the action.

Step 4: Shrink the Distance

One of the biggest ADHD roadblocks is "activation energy": the invisible effort it takes to *start*. If supplies are far away, packed too tightly, or hidden in containers, your brain is more likely to give up.

Anchors reduce activation energy by shrinking the distance between the impulse and the action:

- Keep laundry baskets in multiple rooms.
- Place trash bins wherever clutter tends to collect.
- Have cleaning kits in the bathroom, kitchen, and living room.
- Store art supplies on the table if you want to draw more often.

Remember: the easier it is to start, the more likely it is you'll follow through.

Step 5: Use Color and Contrast

The ADHD brain responds strongly to novelty and stimulation. You can use **color and contrast** as anchors:

- Brightly colored bins for categories (blue = tech cords, red = first aid).
- A neon sticky note on the front door as a reminder to grab lunch.
- A cheerful rug in the entryway to visually anchor the "drop zone."
- Contrasting folders so paperwork categories are instantly recognizable.

Visual pop acts like a mental spotlight, directing your attention where it's needed most.

Step 6: Anchor Habits to Spaces

Every room can have a purpose, and your environment can remind you of it.

- **Kitchen:** Clear counters = meal prep anchor. Put a fruit bowl front-and-center.
- **Living Room:** Remote stored in a tray = cue to reset space after TV time.
- **Bedroom:** Hamper near the bed = clothes don't end up on the floor.
- **Bathroom:** Skincare products laid out in order = visual routine guide.

The point is not to make spaces picture-perfect, but to **make them functional prompts** for the habits you care about.

ADHD-Friendly Environmental Hacks

1. **Double Up:** Keep duplicates of frequently used items (scissors, chargers, cleaning wipes) in multiple locations. It's cheaper than the stress of losing them.

2. **Drop Zones Everywhere:** Trays, baskets, or hooks where items naturally land. Better to contain than constantly fight habits.

3. **See-Through Storage:** Use transparent containers so nothing becomes "invisible clutter."

4. **Label Everything:** Even if it feels silly, labels reinforce memory. "Pens" on the pen jar. "Snacks" on the pantry bin.

5. **Portable Kits:** A cleaning caddy, art kit, or office box that can move room-to-room keeps tasks flexible.

Common Pitfalls (and Fixes)

- **Pitfall:** "I set up anchors, but now it just feels like clutter."
  - **Fix:** Anchors must be intentional. Choose visible *but limited* items. Rotate or reset monthly.
- **Pitfall:** "I forget the anchor exists after a while."
  - **Fix:** Refresh anchors by changing their color, position, or style to re-capture attention.
- **Pitfall:** "My family doesn't use the anchors."
  - **Fix:** Involve them in setup. If they help design the drop zone or choose the bin colors, they're more likely to engage.

Real-Life Example: Jason's Entryway Chaos

Jason's mornings were a mess. Every day, he lost precious minutes searching for his keys, wallet, or work badge. He'd leave the house frazzled, often forgetting something important.

His fix was an **entryway anchor system**: a tray for wallet and keys, a hook for the badge, and a basket for outgoing mail. He even added a sticky note on the door that read: "Keys. Wallet. Badge."

Within a week, his mornings felt calmer. The anchor system didn't change his ADHD, it changed his environment so his ADHD brain didn't have to remember everything.

Step 7: Refresh Regularly

ADHD brains crave novelty. Anchors that work today may fade into the background in a few months. That's normal.

To keep them effective:

- Rotate bins or swap their colors.
- Move anchors slightly to make them noticeable again.
- Do a quick monthly reset of your hotspots (entryway, desk, kitchen counter).

Think of it as *updating your environment to keep up with your brain.*

Closing Thought

Environmental anchors aren't about perfection. They're about **partnership**—letting your space support your brain instead of sabotaging it. By turning your environment into a silent coach, you lower the mental load, reduce forgotten steps, and make routines feel almost automatic.

You don't have to fight your ADHD in the abstract. You can build homes, systems, and cues that quietly whisper: *"Do this next."* And when your space is on your side, consistency becomes possible, not because you forced it, but because it's built right into the world around you.

Reflection Questions:

- *We've gone over a lot in these first few chapters, so if it feels a bit overwhelming, that's okay. Let's pause for a moment and reflect. Which one of the core principles from Book 1, redefining your relationship with clutter, embracing a "good enough" mindset, or the power of small wins, resonates with you the most, and why?*
- *Now, let's put it into practice. What is one specific, tiny change you can make today to begin building your own custom-built system? This could be a 10-minute tidy in one small area or using the two-minute rule for a single task.*

- *In the spirit of embracing a "good enough" mindset, what is one area of your home that you can stop striving for perfection in, and what would a "good enough" version of that space look like for you this week?*

- *Think about the concept of "cognitive load". What is one visual "chaos hotspot" in your home that you know is silently draining your mental energy? What is one single item you can remove or put away from that space to reduce that load?*

- *We discussed redefining our relationship with clutter from a "mess" to an "opportunity." What is one item you've been avoiding or feeling shame about that you can now look at as an opportunity to create a system that works for you?*

This chapter, and this entire book, is a toolkit for a journey of discovery. By giving yourself permission to be imperfect, to be flexible, and to be yourself, you are building a foundation for a life that is not just organized, but also authentic and joyful.

BOOK TWO:

MASTERING ROUTINES AND HABIT FORMATION

CHAPTER 1:

MORNINGS THAT WORK FOR YOUR BRAIN: STARTING THE DAY WITH ENERGY AND FOCUS.

For many with ADHD, mornings can feel like a chaotic race against the clock. The brain fog, the forgotten items, the impulsive detours, it's a recipe for a stressful start to the day. This is a direct result of **executive dysfunction**, a core feature of ADHD that impairs the brain's ability to plan, prioritize, and initiate tasks. The prefrontal cortex (PFC), the brain's "command center" responsible for these skills, relies heavily on neurotransmitters like dopamine and norepinephrine. In the ADHD brain, the dysregulation of these chemicals makes it difficult for the PFC to function optimally, especially after a night of sleep when motivation and focus are at their lowest.

The purpose of a morning routine, therefore, isn't to create a rigid, military-style schedule. Instead, it's to build a predictable, supportive structure that acts as an **external brain**, reducing friction and freeing up mental energy for the day ahead. By automating low-effort habits, you bypass the need for constant, deliberate decision-making, which is a major source of morning stress. The goal is to move from a place of frantic reaction to one of intentional action.

Combatting Brain Fog

The feeling of "brain fog" is a common morning symptom of ADHD, characterized by a sluggish mind and difficulty concentrating. This sensation is directly linked to low levels of dopamine and sluggish blood flow to the brain upon waking. A simple solution is to get your body moving. Physical activity is one of the most effective and accessible ways to stimulate the brain.

Start with something simple that gets your body moving. This could be a five-minute stretch, a glass of water, or a short walk. The physical activity helps to increase blood flow to the brain, which in turn stimulates the release of key neurotransmitters. **Dopamine**, the "feel-good" and "motivation" chemical, gets a boost, as does **norepinephrine**, which helps with focus and arousal. This neurochemical kickstart is a proactive way to reduce brain fog and improve cognitive function before your day even begins.

Consider making these small movements part of your routine: a quick yoga flow, a few minutes of jumping jacks, or even just dancing to a favorite song while you get ready. The key is that the activity is low-effort and enjoyable enough that you'll actually do it. Pairing this with a glass of water also helps to rehydrate your brain and body, which have been without fluids all night.

Preventing Forgotten Items: The "Launchpad"

Forgetting keys, a wallet, or a packed lunch is a classic ADHD challenge, and it's deeply connected to issues with working memory and object permanence. The brain struggles to consistently hold onto the location of objects over time. When you're rushing in the morning, a forgotten item can lead to a frantic, last-minute search that completely derails your calm start.

The solution is to create a physical, non-negotiable external system: the **Launchpad**. This is a designated spot, a small table, a hook, a basket, near your front door where you place everything you need for the day (keys, wallet, phone, bag, lunch). By making this a habit the night before, you completely eliminate the frantic morning search. You are offloading the mental task of remembering where your things are to a reliable, physical system. This strategy works because it removes the reliance on an inconsistent internal system (your working memory) and replaces it with a simple, visual cue. When you wake up, everything is exactly where it should be.

Make it a part of your evening routine to place your items on the Launchpad before you wind down for the night. This is a simple, two-minute habit that pays dividends in reduced morning anxiety and a smoother transition out the door.

Simplifying Decisions

Every decision, no matter how small, depletes mental energy and contributes to **decision fatigue**. For the ADHD brain, which already has a limited supply of this energy, a morning full of choices can be incredibly draining. The act of choosing what to wear, what to eat, or what to do first is a silent burden on the brain's executive functions.

The key to a peaceful morning is to structure your routine so that you're making as few decisions as possible. This involves front-loading the decision-making process into the previous evening when you have less time pressure and more cognitive energy.

- **Lay Out Your Clothes:** A simple act like picking out your clothes the night before removes one major decision from your morning.
- **Pre-Pack Your Lunch:** Packing your lunch after dinner means you don't have to think about it in the morning, saving you time and mental energy.
- **Ready-to-Go Coffee:** Have your coffee machine pre-set and ready to brew with the press of a button.

The less you have to think about, the smoother your morning will be. This isn't about being a robot; it's about intentionally removing low-stakes decisions from a time when your brain is least equipped to handle them. This proactive approach allows you to conserve your precious mental resources for the more complex challenges and tasks that await you later in the day.

Remember, a routine doesn't have to be perfect. The goal is progress, not perfection. If you can only manage two or three of these steps on a given day, that's still a win. The consistency of these small wins will build a foundation for more peaceful, productive mornings and, ultimately, a more organized and less chaotic life.

CHAPTER 2:

THE EVENING RESET: WAKING UP TO A HOME (AND MIND) THAT'S ALREADY READY.

Just as a morning routine sets you up for the day, an evening routine sets you up for a successful tomorrow. For many with ADHD, evenings can be a time of heightened distraction, where the mental energy used for executive functioning throughout the day is depleted. This leads to what some researchers call the **"rebound effect,"** where the brain, tired from a day of constant effort to stay on task, seeks immediate gratification and falls prey to distractions like social media, television, or impulsive projects. A simple task like putting away dishes can turn into an hour-long scroll through social media, leaving you feeling more disorganized and stressed than before.

An evening reset is a series of simple habits designed to bring a sense of closure to the day and proactively prepare your mind and space for the next one. It's a low-effort, high-impact routine that creates a crucial buffer between the chaos of the day and the restorative power of sleep. By engaging in these intentional actions, you are essentially telling your future self, "I've got you covered."

The "Five-Minute Tidy"

The first step in an evening reset is the **"Five-Minute Tidy."** This is a quick, concentrated burst of activity designed to combat the buildup of visual clutter that accumulates throughout the day. Set a timer for five minutes and quickly put away anything that's out of place in your main living areas. The rules are simple:

1. **Don't get sidetracked:** The goal is not a deep clean, but a quick surface reset.

2. **Focus on high-traffic areas:** Prioritize the kitchen counter, living room coffee table, or entryway. These are the spaces that will have the biggest impact on your morning mindset.

3. **Use the "home" principle:** Put items back where they belong, and don't get bogged down in finding new storage solutions.

The psychological power of this small habit is immense. Waking up to a clear, calm space, rather than a messy one, significantly reduces morning anxiety and decision fatigue. A cluttered environment acts as a constant, low-grade stressor, and eliminating it before bed ensures that your brain isn't starting the day in a state of overwhelm. It's an act of compassion for your future self, providing a sense of order before the day's challenges even begin.

The Launchpad Check

Building on the morning routine, the next crucial step is the **"Launchpad Check."** This simple act of preparation is one of the most powerful things you can do to reduce morning stress, which is often a direct result of the ADHD brain's challenges with working memory. After a long day, your brain's ability to hold onto key information is at its lowest. This is why a simple task like remembering your wallet can feel impossible in the morning rush.

The Launchpad, a designated spot near your front door, becomes a physical "external brain." During your evening reset, take a moment to place everything you'll need for the next day on this spot. This includes keys, wallet, phone, work bag, and anything else essential. By consistently doing this, you are offloading the mental burden of remembering these items from your working memory to a simple, visual, and physical system. This not only prevents the frantic morning search but also frees up mental energy for more important tasks.

The Mindful Transition

For many with ADHD, the end of the day is when our minds race the most. The brain, now without the structured stimulation of work or daily tasks, can get caught in a whirlwind of thoughts, worries, and to-do lists, making it difficult to fall asleep. This is because the **sympathetic nervous system** (the "fight or flight" response) is still active, and you need to engage the **parasympathetic nervous system** (the "rest and digest" response) to wind down.

The mindful transition is a series of calming activities that help to quiet your mind and signal to your brain that it's time to rest. This is not about being productive; it's about being intentional.

- **Journaling:** A quick brain dump of all the thoughts swirling in your head can be a powerful way to externalize worries and clear your mind.
- **Reading:** Picking up a physical book (not on a screen) for just 10-15 minutes can help to shift your focus away from the day's stressors.
- **Mindful Listening:** Listening to a calming podcast or a guided meditation can gently redirect your attention and soothe your nervous system.

This evening transition is an act of self-care that tells your brain it's okay to let go. By consistently preparing for the next day and intentionally winding down, you're not just organizing your home, you're organizing your peace of mind and investing in a more restorative night's sleep.

CHAPTER 3:

WEEKEND POWER HOURS: TACKLING BIGGER TASKS WITHOUT THE BURNOUT.

The idea of tackling a "weekend deep dive" can sound exhausting, especially if you're already feeling overwhelmed. For the ADHD brain, a whole day dedicated to cleaning can be a trap. It's a task so big and unstructured that it often triggers **task paralysis**, where the sheer scale of the project prevents it from ever being started. This is due to executive function challenges, particularly with task initiation and the ability to maintain sustained attention. The brain looks at the monumental task, sees no clear starting or stopping point, and simply shuts down.

This chapter is about reframing the deep dive not as a marathon, but as a series of targeted sprints. It's a strategy for tackling large, overwhelming projects by breaking them into manageable, rewarding chunks. The goal is to make significant progress without burning out or abandoning the project entirely.

The Key to Success: Planning and Chunking

The key to a successful weekend deep dive is to proactively create a plan that works with your brain, not against it. This involves two core principles: **Themed Days** and **Time-Chunking**.

Themed Days Instead of a general "cleaning day," which is a recipe for decision fatigue, try a "Kitchen Day" or a "Bedroom Day." This simple act of pre-planning reduces the number of decisions you have to make on the day itself. When you wake up, you don't have to ask, "What should I clean first?" The answer is already decided. This focuses all your energy on a single area, allowing for a more streamlined and less overwhelming experience.

For example, a "Kitchen Day" could involve a series of smaller, themed sprints: "Pantry Organization," "Refrigerator Deep Clean," and "Countertop Declutter." By grouping similar tasks together, you minimize the mental switching costs and can build a productive rhythm.

Time-Chunking This is where you turn your deep dive from a marathon into a series of short, manageable sprints. The **Pomodoro Technique**, a well-known time-management method, is highly effective for the ADHD brain. The technique involves breaking work into 25-minute intervals, separated by short breaks. For a weekend deep dive, you can modify this slightly: break your deep dive into 20-30 minute sprints with built-in breaks.

- Use a timer to stay on task, and when the timer goes off, get up and do something completely different for 10-15 minutes. This honors your brain's need for novelty and helps to replenish your mental energy.
- The structured intervals provide a clear finish line for each task, which gives you a small, immediate sense of accomplishment and a crucial **dopamine hit**. This positive feedback loop is a powerful motivator for the ADHD brain.
- By taking a break, you are preventing the burnout that comes from prolonged focus. This ensures that you can sustain your effort over a longer period without losing momentum.

The Power of an Accountability Partner

Trying to tackle a big project alone can be a major source of procrastination. The ADHD brain thrives on external motivation and social engagement. Having an accountability partner can be a game-changer. The simple act of telling someone your plan, and knowing they'll check in on you, creates a powerful sense of obligation. This is rooted in social psychology, where the desire to not disappoint another person can be a stronger motivator than our own internal desires.

Ask a friend or family member to help you for a few hours, or simply ask them to check in on your progress. Having someone else involved can be a huge motivator.

- **Co-working:** If you have the option, ask a friend or family member to physically help you. The social aspect can make a tedious task feel more like a fun activity.
- **Virtual Check-ins:** If that's not possible, a simple text exchange can be a powerful tool. Let them know what you're working on, and have them send you a quick "How's it going?" text at the end of a sprint.

The All-or-Nothing Trap

It's crucial to remember the goal isn't to clean the entire house in one weekend. The goal is to make significant progress in one or two key areas. By reframing the deep dive as a series of manageable chunks with built-in breaks and support, you can make a weekend deep dive feel less like a chore and more like a productive, achievable project.

This approach directly counters the **all-or-nothing thinking** that so often derails the ADHD brain. The feeling of "I didn't finish everything, so I failed" is replaced with, "I completed my two sprints today, and that's a win." This focus on progress, not perfection, is the foundation for a sustainable, compassionate approach to organization. You're not fighting against your brain; you're working with it to create a system that allows you to succeed.

CHAPTER 4:

THE "BRAIN DUMP" RESET: CLEARING MENTAL CLUTTER SO YOU CAN ACTUALLY RELAX.

Our brains are not designed to be filing cabinets. For those with ADHD, a brain full of to-do lists, ideas, and worries can feel like a crowded, noisy room. This constant internal chatter is a major source of anxiety and a significant barrier to focus. The "brain dump" is a simple yet revolutionary tool for capturing these mental fragments and clearing your mind. It's a proactive strategy to externalize your thoughts, which is a core skill for managing ADHD symptoms.

The concept is rooted in the neurobiology of **working memory**. Working memory is the system in the brain that holds and processes information needed to carry out complex cognitive tasks. For the ADHD brain, working memory is often a limited resource. Every uncompleted task, every looming worry, every fleeting idea consumes a portion of this limited capacity. It's like having too many programs running at once on a computer; everything slows down, and eventually, the system crashes. A brain dump is a way to close those mental tabs and free up your working memory for the task at hand.

How to Perform a Brain Dump

A brain dump is the process of writing down every thought, idea, and task that is swirling in your head. It's about externalizing, not organizing. The process is quick, unfiltered, and designed to minimize the cognitive effort required to start.

1. **Find a Dedicated Space:** The tool itself doesn't matter; the consistency does. Use a notebook, a blank document on your computer, or a notes app on your phone. Having a dedicated space ensures you always know where to go when you feel overwhelmed. This removes the decision of "where do I write this down?" and streamlines the process.

2. **Set a Timer:** Give yourself 5-10 minutes to write down everything that comes to mind. The time limit is crucial for the ADHD brain. It prevents you from getting bogged down in trying to make the dump perfect. It creates a sense of urgency that helps you overcome the initial inertia of starting.

3. **Don't Filter:** Write down everything, no matter how big or small. This could include tasks, worries, creative ideas, grocery lists, or things you need to remember to buy. The key is to suspend judgment and just let the thoughts flow from your brain to the page. There are no bad ideas or trivial worries in a brain dump. The goal is to get it out, not to evaluate it. This unfiltered approach is what truly allows you to clear your mind.

4. **Put It Away:** Once the timer goes off, close the notebook or minimize the window. The goal is to clear your mind, not to immediately start working on everything you wrote down. By closing the document, you are physically signaling to your brain that the information has been captured and it is now safe to forget about it. This is a powerful act of trust in your external system.

The Neuro-Psychological Benefits

The beauty of the brain dump is that it allows you to let go of a thought without having to act on it immediately. You know it's been captured, so your brain can stop looping it in the background. This frees up working memory and reduces the mental clutter that prevents you from focusing on the task at hand.

For the ADHD brain, which struggles with object permanence (the idea that things continue to exist even when they cannot be perceived), a brain dump provides a sense of certainty. When a thought is on the page, you can trust that it is "safe" and will be there when you need it. This reduces the low-grade anxiety of feeling like you might forget something important.

The act of writing is also a powerful tool for grounding the mind. The physical act of putting pen to paper can be a form of mindfulness, helping you to slow down and connect with your thoughts in a more deliberate way. It moves your thoughts from the abstract, chaotic space of your mind into a concrete, organized form on a page. This externalization is the first and most critical step toward bringing order to your internal world.

In summary, a brain dump is not just an organizational tool; it's a mental health practice. It's a way to give your overworked brain a break, to offload its burdens, and to create the mental space you need to focus, create, and live with less anxiety.

CHAPTER 5:

HARNESSING HYPERFOCUS: TURNING YOUR ADHD SUPERPOWER INTO A DEEP-CLEANING TOOL.

Hyperfocus is one of the most powerful and misunderstood aspects of ADHD. It's the ability to lock onto a task with intense concentration, often for hours at a time, to the exclusion of everything else. While hyperfocus is often associated with playing video games or diving deep into a new hobby, it can be a superpower for organization and cleaning. This unique ability is a direct result of the ADHD brain's dopamine-seeking nature. When a task is novel, challenging, and engaging, it provides a powerful dopamine hit that allows for an extraordinary level of sustained attention. Instead of viewing hyperfocus as a flaw, this chapter is about learning to intentionally trigger and harness it to your advantage.

The Conditions for Hyperfocus

Hyperfocus is a phenomenon you can't force, but you can actively create the conditions that make it more likely to occur. It is often triggered by a combination of interest, challenge, and a sense of urgency. By intentionally cultivating these conditions, you can transform a daunting cleaning task into a rewarding project.

- **Interest:** Choose a task that is genuinely interesting to you. This might be organizing a collection, rearranging furniture, or tackling a complex digital filing system. The key is to find the angle that sparks curiosity. If you love history, maybe you organize your old family photos. If you're a tech enthusiast, perhaps you focus on re-wiring and organizing all the cables behind your entertainment center.

- **Challenge:** Turn the task into a game. Can you organize your entire closet in one hour? Can you make your pantry look like a professional grocery store in 45 minutes? By introducing a time limit or a specific, measurable goal, you're tapping into the brain's desire for a challenge. This activates the reward system, releasing dopamine and making the task more engaging.

- **Urgency:** Create a soft deadline to add a sense of importance. Tell a friend you're going to show them your organized closet in two hours. Having an external commitment, even a small one, provides the kind of social pressure that can be a powerful motivator for the ADHD brain.

The Activation Phase

Don't wait for hyperfocus to strike; actively seek it out. This is where the strategies from earlier chapters come into play, particularly the concept of lowering the barrier to entry. The biggest hurdle is often the activation energy required to start.

Start by eliminating all distractions. Put your phone in another room, turn off non-essential notifications, and turn on some music (without lyrics if they're distracting). Music is an incredibly powerful tool for the ADHD brain, as it can act as a form of "auditory scaffolding," providing a consistent external stimulus that helps to focus the mind and override the constant internal chatter.

Commit to just starting the task for five minutes. This small, non-threatening commitment is often enough to trigger the hyperfocus. The act of starting, even without a perfect plan, can quickly become an immersive experience. This is a crucial neuro-psychological trick: the initial effort is a small, low-risk investment that often pays off with a burst of high-reward, focused activity.

The Landing Pad and Post-Hyperfocus Care

The downside of hyperfocus is that when it ends, you can feel utterly exhausted and overwhelmed. The intense concentration required for a hyperfocused state can deplete key neurotransmitters like dopamine and serotonin, leading to a sudden "crash" or feeling of burnout. In this state, the mess you created in your wake can feel like a new, even more daunting problem.

To prepare for this, set up a **"landing pad"** for when your hyperfocus ends. This is a small, clear space, a box, a corner of a table, or a simple basket, where you can put down any tools, half-organized items, or general clutter. This simple act of pre-planning prevents the post-hyperfocus crash from creating a new mess. It gives you a safe, designated spot to drop everything without creating a new source of visual clutter. When you're ready, you can come back to it.

Furthermore, it's essential to plan for your recovery. After a deep hyperfocus session, your brain is exhausted.

- **Rehydrate and refuel:** You may have forgotten to eat or drink.
- **Take a planned rest:** Lie down, take a walk, or do something completely non-demanding for at least 30 minutes to give your brain a chance to reset.
- **Acknowledge your effort:** Give yourself a moment to acknowledge the significant work you just completed. This conscious celebration provides a final dopamine reward that reinforces the positive behavior.

By learning to harness this unique strength, you can turn a daunting cleaning project into a productive and even enjoyable experience. You're not fighting against your brain's nature; you're using it as a powerful tool to build the life you want.

CHAPTER 6:

THE TWO-MINUTE CONTAINER RULE: KEEPING CLUTTER IN CHECK AUTOMATICALLY

Why Containers Are Secretly Powerful

If you live with ADHD, clutter often feels like a sneaky enemy. You don't set out to pile things on the counter, but suddenly there's a stack of unopened mail, a few receipts, a random pen, and yesterday's coffee mug. Multiply that across your home and it can feel like chaos spreads faster than you can ever clean it up.

Here's the good news: clutter is not a moral failing. It's simply **stuff without a clear home**. And when your brain has to make endless micro-decisions about where to put each item ("Does this go in the drawer? On the desk? Back in the bag?"), it gets overwhelmed and defaults to dropping things wherever.

Enter the **container**. A container is an *external system* that does the thinking for you. It tells your brain, "This is where this type of thing lives." Even better, it puts a natural limit on how much of something you can keep before it needs attention.

The **Two-Minute Container Rule** builds on this concept. It's a simple, ADHD-friendly system:

1. **Designate containers for recurring clutter categories.**
2. **When a container is full, take two minutes to reset it.**

That's it. No overwhelming deep-clean, no endless decision fatigue. Containers act as boundaries, and the two-minute reset keeps clutter from turning into chaos.

Why ADHD Brains Love Containers

To see why this works so well, let's look at what containers *actually do* for your brain:

- **Reduce decision fatigue:** You don't have to wonder where mail goes, it goes in the mail basket.
- **Create visual boundaries:** A container makes it obvious when a category has reached its limit.
- **Shrink activation energy:** Tossing keys into a bowl is faster than putting them in a drawer.
- **Anchor habits:** The physical presence of a container becomes a behavioral cue.

In other words, containers externalize memory and reduce friction, two things the ADHD brain desperately needs.

Step 1: Spot Your "Clutter Categories"

Before you start buying bins, pause. You don't need containers for *everything*. The most powerful ones target recurring clutter categories, the items that constantly trip you up.

Look around your home and ask:

- What always piles up on counters?
- What never seems to have a home?
- What do I constantly misplace?

Common ADHD clutter categories include:

- Mail and paperwork
- Keys, wallet, phone, chargers
- Receipts
- Random small items (lip balm, coins, pens)
- Laundry (dirty, clean-but-not-folded, mismatched socks)
- Dishes that migrate to non-kitchen spaces

Each of these deserves its own container.

Step 2: Choose ADHD-Friendly Containers

Not all containers are created equal. If it takes too much effort to use them, your brain will ignore them. Choose containers that:

- **Are open and easy to access.** Lids create friction.
- **Are visible.** Clear bins or open trays beat opaque boxes.
- **Are sized appropriately.** Too big = a black hole. Too small = constant overflow.
- **Match your natural habits.** If you always drop mail by the door, put the mail basket *there*, not across the room.

Examples:

- A wide, shallow tray for keys and wallet.
- A wire basket for incoming mail.
- A small laundry hamper in the bedroom *and* bathroom.
- A pretty bowl on the coffee table for remotes.

The goal isn't Pinterest-perfect aesthetics, it's usability.

Step 3: The Two-Minute Reset

Here's where the magic happens. The **Two-Minute Container Rule** is simple:

- When a container fills up, don't panic.
- Set a timer for two minutes.
- Empty or reset the container.

That's it.

The time limit matters. It reframes the task from "ugh, I have to clean all this" to "I only need two minutes." Even if you don't finish, two minutes is enough to make a dent and prevent the build-up from spiraling.

Examples:

- Mail basket full? Spend two minutes recycling junk mail and pulling out bills.
- Laundry hamper overflowing? Two minutes to start a load.
- Toy bin full? Two minutes to toss broken toys and reset.

By making it short and non-threatening, you sidestep the ADHD trap of perfectionism and procrastination.

Step 4: Use Containers as "Pause Points"

Here's a powerful mindset shift: containers don't have to be permanent homes. They can be **pause points**, temporary holding spots until you have energy to finish.

- A basket on the stairs for items that need to go upstairs.
- A tray on your desk for papers you'll sort later.
- A bin by the door for things to return to friends or stores.

This removes the pressure of "I have to finish this right now" and instead creates a gentle system that moves clutter along in stages.

Step 5: Rotate and Refresh

ADHD brains crave novelty, so containers can fade into the background if they stay the same forever. To keep them effective:

- Change the color or style seasonally.
- Re-label bins every few months.
- Swap positions to make them noticeable again.

This refresh re-engages your attention and keeps the system working long-term.

Real-Life Example: Maya's Mail Mountain

Maya dreaded her mail. She'd toss it on the kitchen counter, where it snowballed into intimidating stacks. She'd avoid it for weeks, then panic when bills were overdue.

Her fix? A **mail basket by the door**. Every piece of mail went in immediately. Twice a week, she set a timer for two minutes and sorted: recycle junk, put bills in a "to pay" folder, file the rest.

Suddenly, mail wasn't a mountain. It was a five-minute task spread across the week.

Step 6: Pair Containers with Routines

Containers work best when linked to small, regular habits.

- Empty the entryway tray while your coffee brews.
- Sort the mail basket every Tuesday and Friday.
- Reset the laundry hamper every Saturday morning.
- Clear the "miscellaneous" basket before bedtime.

These mini-routines take minutes but prevent weeks of stress later.

ADHD-Friendly Hacks for Containers

1. **Label Everything.** Even obvious bins. Labels remove the micro-step of thinking.

2. **Double Up.** If clutter piles in multiple spots, put containers in *each* one.

3. **Match Flow, Not Theory.** Place containers where the clutter naturally happens, not where you wish it would.

4. **Use Pretty Ones (If You Care).** A container you like looking at is one you'll actually use.

5. **Don't Over-Organize.** Categories can be broad. "Mail." "Tech." "Random stuff." Keep it simple.

Common Pitfalls (and Fixes)

- **Pitfall:** "My containers just became more clutter."
  - **Fix:** Remember the Two-Minute Reset. Containers are holding spots, not dumping grounds.
- **Pitfall:** "I forget to empty the containers."
  - **Fix:** Add container resets to your Reminder Web (see Chapter 7). Use phone alarms or sticky notes.
- **Pitfall:** "I made my system too complicated."
  - **Fix:** Simplify categories. Broad bins are better than micro-sorted chaos.

The Psychology of "Enough"

Containers also teach a subtle but important lesson: the power of *enough*. If your book basket is full, maybe it's time to stop buying new ones until you read the old ones. If your snack bin is overflowing, maybe it's time to finish what you have.

This isn't about restriction, it's about creating natural, external boundaries so your brain doesn't have to constantly police your behavior. The container does it for you.

Closing Thought

The **Two-Minute Container Rule** isn't glamorous. It won't make your home look like a magazine. But that's not the goal. The goal is to make your environment easier to live in, one basket, one tray, one boundary at a time.

When you externalize memory into containers and pair them with tiny resets, you take the pressure off your brain and let your space work for you. Over time, these little systems add up to something powerful: a home that stays livable, not because you forced yourself to be perfect, but because you designed it to support your ADHD brain.

And that's the beauty of external systems. They don't demand discipline—they create ease.

CHAPTER 7:

THE REMINDER WEB: BUILDING A NETWORK OF SUPPORTS THAT REMEMBER FOR YOU

Why a Single Reminder Isn't Enough

You've probably experienced this: you set one phone alarm to remind you to take your medication at 8 AM. The alarm goes off. You silence it. You tell yourself you'll get up in a minute. Then three hours later, you realize you never took the medication.

This isn't laziness, it's ADHD neurology. Our brains are **brilliant at responding to novelty and stimulation** but **terrible at holding future intentions in working memory**. A single reminder is fragile. If you miss it, get distracted, or override it, the whole system collapses.

That's why you need a **Reminder Web**. Instead of one fragile thread, you create a *network of cues* that catch you from multiple angles. If you ignore one, another is waiting. If you miss the second, the third picks up the slack. The web doesn't rely on your memory, it holds you gently but firmly in place.

The ADHD Problem with "Just Remembering"

Psychologists call ADHD an **executive functioning disorder**, meaning the brain struggles with self-management skills like planning, sequencing, and remembering. For many of us, intentions are like soap bubbles, they're beautiful for a moment, then they vanish.

That's why you can genuinely *mean* to pay the bill, fold the laundry, or take the trash out, and still not do it. Memory alone is too leaky to trust.

External reminders are not a crutch. They are a **prosthetic for working memory**. Just as someone with weak eyesight uses glasses, someone with ADHD can use reminders to strengthen recall.

What Is the Reminder Web?

The Reminder Web is a layered system of **redundant reminders** that:

1. **Externalize memory.** The web holds the task so your brain doesn't have to.

2. **Reduce failure points.** If you miss one reminder, another catches you.

3. **Work across modalities.** Visual, auditory, physical, and social cues all reinforce each other.

4. **Create momentum.** Repeated nudges gently guide you toward action instead of demanding discipline.

Think of it like having safety nets under a trapeze. One net is risky. A whole web of nets? Much safer.

Step 1: Map Your "Memory Leaks"

Before you build your web, notice where tasks currently slip through the cracks.

Ask yourself:

- What do I *always* forget?
- When during the day do I get derailed?
- Which reminders have failed me before (and why)?

Examples:

- Forgetting meds because the pill bottle is in a closed cabinet.
- Forgetting laundry because it's out of sight in the basement.
- Forgetting appointments because one phone alert wasn't loud enough.

These leaks are the places your web needs to be strongest.

Step 2: Layer Your Reminders

A Reminder Web works because it layers cues. Instead of hoping one will stick, you create **redundancy**.

Example: Morning Medication

- Phone alarm at 8:00 AM.
- Pill bottle on the nightstand (visual cue).
- Post-it note on the bathroom mirror ("Take meds").
- Smart speaker reminder at 8:15 if you haven't logged it.
- Accountability text from a friend once a week.

Now, missing your meds would require ignoring *five* reminders, not just one.

Step 3: Use Multiple Modalities

Different types of reminders work on different brain pathways. A strong web uses a mix:

- **Visual:** Sticky notes, wall calendars, whiteboards, color-coded bins.
- **Auditory:** Phone alarms, smart speakers, kitchen timers, music cues.
- **Physical:** Placing items in your path (trash bag on the doorknob).
- **Digital:** Calendar notifications, task apps, recurring checklists.

- **Social:** Accountability buddies, shared family reminders, coworking groups.

The more modalities you use, the more resilient your web becomes.

Step 4: Make Reminders Unignorable

ADHD brains are experts at tuning out background noise. The trick is to make reminders stand out.

- Use novelty: Rotate alarm sounds or sticky note colors.
- Use location: Place cues in spots you literally can't miss.
- Use humor: Write silly or exaggerated notes ("Hey genius, water the plants!").
- Use redundancy: Pair alarms with physical cues so it's harder to ignore.

Unignorable doesn't mean overwhelming. It means designing reminders that cut through the fog in ways that feel supportive, not nagging.

Step 5: Automate Wherever Possible

One of the best parts of the Reminder Web is automation. The less effort you spend remembering to remind yourself, the better.

- **Digital automation:** Set recurring calendar alerts, auto-bill pay, and recurring grocery orders.
- **Smart home automation:** Lights that dim at bedtime, plugs that turn off appliances, thermostats that adjust.
- **Physical automation:** Drop zones (keys always in the bowl, mail always in the basket).

Automation creates a background structure that runs without you having to constantly think about it.

Step 6: Pair Reminders with Routines

Reminders work best when anchored to existing habits.

- Put your vitamin bottle next to your coffee maker (cue = morning coffee).
- Put your gym shoes by the front door (cue = leaving the house).

- Add a calendar alert to check the mail on the same day you take out the trash.

The Reminder Web isn't just about nudges, it's about weaving them into the natural flow of your day.

Step 7: Refresh Your Web Regularly

Here's the catch: ADHD brains adapt quickly. What feels novel today becomes invisible in a few weeks. That's why you need to refresh your web:

- Change alarm tones monthly.
- Rotate sticky note colors or locations.
- Swap your whiteboard for a chalkboard or digital screen.
- Update accountability partners or groups.

Refreshing keeps your web visible and effective long-term.

Real-Life Example: Sarah's Laundry Loop

Sarah constantly forgot her laundry in the washer. Clothes would sit for days, start to smell, and need rewashing.

She built a Reminder Web:

- Phone alarm labeled "Switch Laundry" whenever she started a load.
- A sticky note on the washing machine lid: "Don't forget me!"
- A smart plug set to turn off the washer light after 90 minutes.
- A text check-in with her roommate once a week.

Within a month, she stopped re-washing loads. Her web caught her before the task slipped away.

ADHD-Friendly Reminder Hacks

1. **Name Your Alarms.** Instead of "8:00 AM," label it "Take Meds" or "Start Dishwasher."

2. **Use Visual Landmines.** Place items in your way so you literally can't forget.

3. **Double-Cue Important Tasks.** Always pair a digital reminder with a physical cue.

4. **Leverage Other People's Brains.** Ask friends or family for gentle nudges.

5. **Stack Reminders with Rewards.** Pair reminders with something pleasant (music, coffee, small break).

Common Pitfalls (and Fixes)

- **Pitfall:** "I ignore my reminders after a week."
  - o **Fix:** Refresh regularly with new sounds, colors, or placements.
- **Pitfall:** "I feel nagged by my own systems."
  - o **Fix:** Keep tone playful and kind. Reminders should feel like support, not shame.
- **Pitfall:** "Too many reminders make me overwhelmed."
  - o **Fix:** Start with one strong web for your biggest pain point, then expand gradually.

The Psychology of Redundancy

You might worry that needing multiple reminders makes you "weak" or "childish." Let's flip that.

Airplanes have multiple backup systems. Doctors use checklists. Athletes have coaches. Professionals in every field use redundancy because it *works*.

For ADHD, redundancy isn't overkill—it's wisdom. The Reminder Web is how you build consistency without relying on unreliable memory or discipline.

Closing Thought

A single reminder is like a single thread—fragile, easy to snap. But a web of reminders? That's strong, resilient, forgiving. It doesn't demand perfection. It doesn't punish you for forgetting. It simply catches you, gently, again and again.

When you build a Reminder Web, you stop relying on shaky memory and start relying on systems. And that's the true power of external supports: they let your environment, your technology, and your community carry what your brain was never designed to hold alone.

You don't have to "just remember." You can build a web that remembers *for you.*

Reflection Questions:

- *In Book 2, we discussed several strategies for creating routines and habits. Which of these, either the morning routine, the evening reset, or the weekend deep dive, do you think would have the most immediate positive impact on your life? What is one specific, tiny action you can take this week to begin implementing it?*

- *This book also introduced the "Brain Dump" and the idea of harnessing hyperfocus. What is one specific task, either a small cleaning project or an organizational challenge, that you feel you could use a "Brain Dump" on, or intentionally engage your hyperfocus to complete this week?*

- *Think about the concept of the **"evening reset"**. What is one item or uncompleted task that, when left undone at the end of the day, consistently causes you stress or anxiety the next morning? How could a simple, five-minute evening habit prevent this?*

- *We discussed how to **harness hyperfocus**. What is a hobby or activity you've hyperfocused on in the past? What were the conditions of that experience (music, a challenge, no distractions) and how could you intentionally replicate those conditions for a productive task this week?*

- *The purpose of these routines isn't just to clean, but to create a specific feeling. What is the feeling or mental state you're hoping to achieve with a more consistent routine (e.g., peace, calm, control)?*

BOOK THREE:

DECLUTTERING AND ORGANIZING MADE EASY

CHAPTER 1:

KEEP, TOSS, DONATE – SIMPLIFIED: A NO-DRAMA FRAMEWORK FOR FAST DECISIONS.

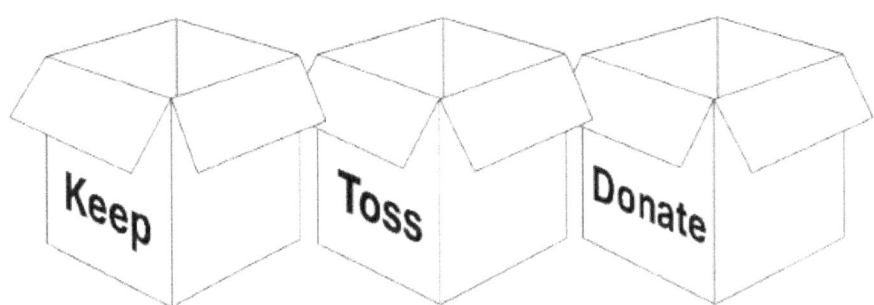

Traditional decluttering methods often fail the ADHD brain because they rely on a single, prolonged session of decision-making. The sheer volume of choices (such as Should I keep this? Will I need it later? Is this still good?) is a surefire recipe for **decision fatigue**. When faced with this cognitive overload, the prefrontal cortex, which is already working overtime to manage focus and attention, becomes exhausted, leading to paralysis and the complete abandonment of the task.

The **"Keep, Toss, Donate"** method is a more manageable and less overwhelming approach that simplifies the process into a clear, three-part framework. It's designed to combat decision fatigue and keep you moving forward by turning a monumental task into a series of small, rapid-fire choices.

The Three Bins: A Simple Framework

To start, you need to set up your decluttering station. Grab three containers:

- A **"Keep"** box for items you want to put in their proper place. This is not their final destination; it's a temporary holding zone. The goal is to get things off the cluttered surface and into a designated box, which is a significant win.

- A **"Toss"** bag for things that are broken, expired, or have no use. This category should be for items that require zero thought. If it's a broken gadget, a holey sock, or an expired condiment, it goes in the bag without a second thought.

- A **"Donate/Sell"** box for items that are still useful but no longer serve you. This re-frames the action. You're not losing something; you're giving it a new life and helping someone else. This positive mental reframing can make the decision much easier.

This three-bin system is a physical representation of the decisions you'll be making, which is a powerful tool for a brain that relies on visual cues.

The Power of Categories

Instead of trying to declutter an entire room at once, a task that has no clear end, break the process down into **categories**. This is a powerful strategy rooted in cognitive science. The brain processes information more efficiently when it's grouped. By focusing on one type of item at a time (e.g., all your shoes, all your books, all your kitchen utensils), you significantly reduce the mental "cost" of switching between different types of items. This makes the task more finite and less daunting.

As you pick up each item, make a quick, intuitive decision: Keep, Toss, or Donate? Don't overthink it. The goal is to make a rapid decision and move on. The first instinct is often the right one. This is a direct counter to analysis paralysis, as it prioritizes momentum over perfect judgment. By the end of a category session, you'll have a clear sense of accomplishment, which provides a crucial **dopamine** hit and motivates you for the next round.

The "Maybe" Box is a Trap

You may be tempted to create a "Maybe" box for items you're unsure about. Avoid this at all costs. A "Maybe" box is a trap for the ADHD brain. It doesn't solve the problem; it simply delays the decision and creates a new form of clutter. It becomes a graveyard of indecision, a physical manifestation of your fear of making the "wrong" choice. This feeds into the very anxiety you're trying to escape.

If you're truly on the fence, lean towards donating. The item will be more useful to someone else than it is collecting dust in your home. If a "Maybe" box is absolutely necessary for your peace of mind, make it a temporary system with a hard deadline. For example, "I'll keep this box for three months, and if I haven't opened it by then, everything inside gets donated." This structure turns a vague, endless "maybe" into a concrete, time-limited decision.

A Practical Application: The Decluttering Sprint

To make this method even more effective, combine it with the **"10-Minute Tidy"** concept from Book 2. This is the **"Decluttering Sprint."**

1. **Set a Timer:** Set a timer for 10-15 minutes. This creates a clear start and a clear end.

2. **Grab Your Bins:** Have your "Keep," "Toss," and "Donate" containers ready.

3. **Choose a Category:** Pick a single, small category to work on, like "all the mugs in the cupboard" or "all the pens on my desk."

4. **Rapid-Fire Decisions:** Work through the items as quickly as you can, making a quick decision for each.

5. **Stop When the Timer Goes Off:** When the timer dings, you're done.

The "Keep, Toss, Donate" method provides a simple, clear-cut framework that turns a huge, overwhelming task into a series of small, rapid-fire decisions. It's not about being perfect; it's about being decisive and making progress. By building this momentum, you can reclaim your space and your peace of mind, one small decision at a time.

CHAPTER 2:

PAPERWORK & DIGITAL CHAOS: SYSTEMS TO CONTROL YOUR INBOX, DESK, AND FILES.

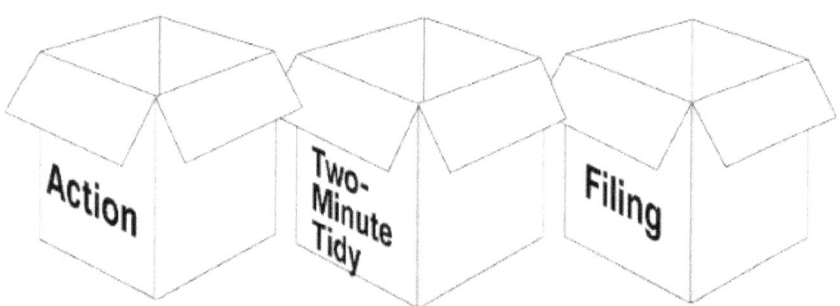

Paperwork and digital files can be a constant source of stress for the ADHD brain. They multiply with seemingly no effort, and the thought of organizing them can feel impossible. This is because both physical and digital clutter trigger the same executive function challenges that make physical clutter so draining: task initiation, prioritization, and working memory. The endless stream of emails, files, and documents competes for your attention, creating a significant **cognitive load** and contributing to a pervasive sense of overwhelm. This chapter provides simple, actionable strategies to create a system that works for the modern, busy individual, turning chaos into order one simple step at a time.

Taming Paperwork

The key to managing paper clutter is to have a simple, visible system that doesn't require a complex mental map. The reason piles form on every available surface is a neuro-psychological one: the brain struggles with object permanence. If an item is in a drawer or a folder, it's easily forgotten. A visible system acts as an external brain, providing a clear, non-negotiable home for every piece of paper that enters your life.

- **The "Action" Box:** All incoming mail and papers go into a single, designated box. This prevents piles from forming on every surface. This "Action" box is not for storage; it is a temporary holding zone. By funnelling all new papers into one spot, you're containing the chaos and creating a single point of entry for all paperwork. This is a fundamental step in reducing the visual clutter that drains your mental energy.

- **The "Two-Minute Tidy":** Once a week, go through the "Action" box. If a piece of paper takes less than two minutes to deal with (e.g., paying a bill online, scheduling an appointment, or signing a form), do it immediately. This is a direct application of the "Two-Minute Rule" from Book 2, which leverages the fact that the mental energy required to put off a simple task is often greater than the energy required to complete it. For items that will take longer, move them to a separate "To Do" file to be scheduled into a longer work block.

- **A Simple Filing System:** For papers you need to keep, create a filing system with broad, easy-to-remember categories. Avoid micro-filing with folders for every single type of document. Instead, use broad categories like **"Medical," "Financial," "Home,"** and **"Important Documents."** The fewer folders you have, the easier it is to maintain, and the less cognitive effort is required to file a new document. A simple box or a hanging file system with clear, large labels works best. The goal is retrieval, not perfection.

Conquering Digital Clutter

Digital clutter can be just as overwhelming and anxiety-inducing as physical clutter. An inbox with thousands of unread emails, a desktop covered in icons, or a downloads folder full of unorganized files is a digital representation of a disorganized mind. It can lead to the same feelings of overwhelm and analysis paralysis.

- **The "Digital Brain Dump":** Just like with physical thoughts, take time to dump all your unorganized files, photos, and digital to-dos into a single, temporary folder. This is a crucial first step that gets everything out of sight and into a single, contained space, reducing visual clutter on your desktop and in your mind. From this folder, you can later organize the files into their proper homes.

- **Email Management:** Your email inbox is a primary source of digital stress. Create a simple **two-folder system**: an "**Action**" folder for emails that need a response and an "**Archive**" folder for everything else. The goal is to get your inbox to zero as often as possible. Once you've read an email and completed any necessary actions, archive it. This simple system, combined with unsubscribing from unnecessary mailing lists, makes managing your inbox a proactive task instead of a reactive one.

- **Desktop Declutter:** Your desktop is your digital workspace. A cluttered desktop makes it difficult to find files and is a constant visual distraction. Keep it clean and use a few folders to group similar items. For example, have a folder for "Current Projects" and another for "Downloads." The principle of a clean workspace from Book 1 applies here just as much as it does to a physical desk.

By creating a simple, easy-to-maintain system for both physical and digital clutter, you can significantly reduce the mental load and anxiety associated with them. The goal is not a pristine, perfect system but a functional one that supports your unique brain.

CHAPTER 3:

TAMING THE CHAOS HOTSPOTS: ADHD-FRIENDLY STRATEGIES FOR KITCHENS, CLOSETS, AND MORE.

Every home has its "chaos hotspots," areas that seem to attract clutter no matter how many times you clean them. For many with ADHD, these are often the kitchen counters, the closet floor, or the bathroom sink. These spots are not a reflection of a personal failing; they are a direct result of a system that is not designed for the ADHD brain. These areas are low-effort landing zones that trigger **visual clutter**, which in turn creates a constant cognitive drain. This chapter provides specific, actionable strategies for taming these trouble spots and creating systems that are intuitive and easy to maintain. The key is to design a system that works *with* your brain's natural tendencies, not against them.

The Kitchen Counter: The Primary Landing Strip

The kitchen counter is often the home's primary landing strip. It's the first place we put down keys, mail, groceries, and miscellaneous items. For a brain that struggles with object permanence (the ability to remember that an item exists even when it's not in sight), the counter becomes a perfect short-term memory substitute. Everything is visible, but the sheer volume of visual information creates a significant **cognitive load**.

To combat this, the goal is to get as much off the counter as possible.

- **Create a Designated Launchpad:** Use a decorative tray or bowl for high-value, high-use items like keys, wallet, and sunglasses. This corrals the clutter into a single, defined space.
- **Go Vertical:** Use magnetic strips on the wall for knives and other metal utensils. Mount a small corkboard or a hanging file on the wall to hold important papers, notes, or bills. This utilizes unused vertical space and keeps the counter clear for its intended purpose: food preparation.
- **Give Appliances a Home:** If you have small appliances you don't use every day, create a home for them in a cupboard. If you use them daily, give them a specific spot on the counter and make it a habit to put them back after each use.

The goal isn't an empty, sterile counter, but a counter clear enough to make dinner without feeling overwhelmed.

The Closet Floor: The Silent Dumping Ground

The closet floor is a common dumping ground because it's a low-effort, out-of-sight space. The "out of sight, out of mind" principle works here in reverse: since the clutter is not visible every day, it can build up to an unmanageable level without triggering a sense of urgency. The moment you open the door and see the mess, it becomes an overwhelming task that is immediately shut away.

To solve this, you need to create a simple, visible system for items that would otherwise end up on the floor.

- **Install Simple Shelving or a Shoe Rack:** This provides a clear, designated home for shoes, which are a major culprit of floor clutter.

- **Utilize Cubbies or Bins:** Use cubbies or labeled bins to create a home for clothes you haven't decided on, or for seasonal items. The visual boundaries of the cubbies help to contain the clutter.

- **Commit to the "One-In, One-Out" Rule:** For every item of clothing you bring into your home, one must leave. This simple rule prevents the closet from reaching a state of critical mass. Make a commitment to put one item away as soon as you take it off. This small habit can prevent the closet floor from becoming a major problem.

The Bathroom Sink: The Jumble of Jars

The bathroom sink and counter often become a jumble of bottles, tubes, and containers. This visual clutter is a subtle but persistent stressor. It also makes a simple task like wiping down the counter feel like a massive undertaking.

- **Use Trays or Small Containers:** Use a simple tray or small containers to group similar items (e.g., all your dental care products, all your skincare). This prevents a jumble of bottles and tubes and makes it easy to wipe down the counter.

- **Go Vertical:** Install a wall-mounted toothbrush holder to get items off the counter.

- **The Power of the Drawer:** Use drawer organizers to provide a specific home for items that don't need to be on the counter. This keeps them accessible but out of sight, providing a sense of visual calm.

The Entryway: The Catch-All Zone

A final, common chaos hotspot is the entryway or mudroom. This space is the first and last point of contact with the outside world, making it a natural catch-all for coats, bags, shoes, and mail.

- **Hooks for Everything:** Install a series of hooks at varying heights for coats, bags, and backpacks. This is a low-effort alternative to a closet and provides an immediate home for items as you walk in the door.

- **A Shoe Rack or Mat:** Give shoes a dedicated spot. This prevents them from being scattered across the floor.
- **A Mail Drop Zone:** Place a small basket or box on a nearby table. All incoming mail goes here, preventing it from being scattered throughout the house. This is the first step in the paperwork system from Chapter 2.

The key to taming chaos hotspots is to design a system that works with your brain's natural tendencies. This isn't about being a neat freak; it's about creating a home that is functional and reduces daily friction. By setting up these simple, intuitive systems, you can dramatically reduce the amount of mental energy you spend on managing your physical space and free up your mind for the things that truly matter.

CHAPTER 4:

THE ONE-IN, ONE-OUT RULE: A SIMPLE HABIT THAT KEEPS CLUTTER FROM CREEPING BACK.

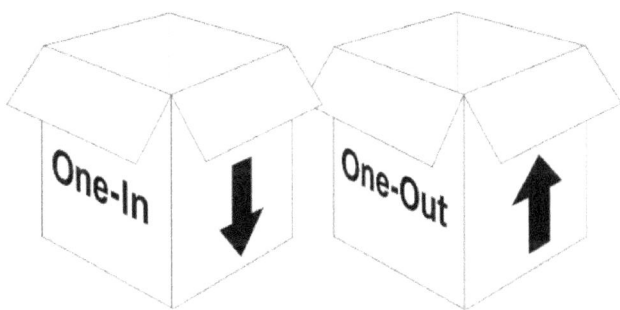

Impulse purchases are a common challenge for those with ADHD, leading to a constant inflow of new items that contribute to clutter. The "One-In, One-Out" rule is a simple, effective method to prevent this cycle and maintain a sense of order in your home. The impulse to acquire new things is often a direct result of the ADHD brain's constant search for **novelty and a dopamine hit**. The excitement of a new purchase provides an immediate, temporary reward that can override a longer-term goal like a tidy home. The "One-In, One-Out" rule is a powerful, proactive strategy that introduces a moment of intentionality, interrupting the impulsive loop and creating a sustainable system for keeping your home organized.

The Rule in Practice

The rule is exactly what it sounds like: for every new item that comes into your home, one similar item must leave. It's a simple, non-negotiable principle that forces you to be mindful of every purchase. This is not about deprivation; it's about conscious acquisition.

- **Clothes:** If you buy a new shirt, you must donate or toss an old one. This forces you to be honest about what you already own and what you actually wear. It transforms a spontaneous trip to the store into a mindful evaluation of your wardrobe. It prevents your closet from overflowing and makes getting dressed in the morning a less overwhelming task.
- **Books:** When you buy a new book, find one on your shelf that you have already read and pass it on to a friend or donate it to a library. This helps you curate a collection of books you truly want to read or reference, rather than a backlog of books that serve as a visual reminder of what you haven't accomplished.
- **Kitchen Gadgets:** If you buy a new kitchen gadget, get rid of an old one you no longer use. This prevents your drawers and cupboards from becoming a graveyard of single-use items you bought with good intentions.
- **Kids' Toys:** When a new toy comes in, one old toy must be passed along. This teaches children the same principle and keeps their play areas manageable.

This method works because it externalizes the decision-making process. The rule is a clear, physical constraint that bypasses the mental gymnastics of whether or not you should make a purchase. It simplifies the decision: "Is this new item worth the cost of getting rid of an old item?"

The Neuro-Psychological Benefits

The "One-In, One-Out" rule is a powerful mental trick. It shifts the focus from the pleasure of a new purchase to the act of mindful exchange. It forces a moment of **intentionality** that can prevent an impulsive buy from becoming a future clutter problem. For a brain that struggles with **impulse control** and long-term planning, this rule provides an essential, built-in filter.

Furthermore, this rule helps to combat the psychological trap of **"out of sight, out of mind."** New items that are not immediately addressed can quickly contribute to a new clutter pile. By forcing an immediate action, removing an old item, you are creating a new habit of maintenance.

The rule also helps you redefine your relationship with your belongings. Instead of seeing them as things you've acquired, you see them as a curated collection that serves a purpose in your life. This mindset shift is crucial for long-term organization.

Addressing Common Challenges

While the rule is simple, implementing it can have its challenges.

- **"What about sentimental items?"** This is a valid concern. The "One-In, One-Out" rule is primarily for everyday, non-sentimental items. For sentimental items, create a small, designated "Memory Box." The rule is that the box has a limited size. Once it's full, you must re-evaluate its contents before adding anything new.

- **"What if I don't have a similar item to get rid of?"** Use a flexible interpretation. The goal is to maintain a balance, not a strict one-to-one ratio. If you buy a new item and can't find a similar one to remove, find something else that is no longer serving you, or commit to a small decluttering sprint to make room.

The "One-In, One-Out" rule is about creating a conscious filter that helps you maintain control over what comes into your home. It's an act of self-care that prevents future overwhelm and supports a calm, organized environment. By embracing this simple habit, you're not lowering your standards; you're setting realistic ones that allow you to thrive.

CHAPTER 5:

FURNITURE & STORAGE THAT WORK FOR YOU: DESIGNING SPACES YOUR BRAIN CAN ACTUALLY MAINTAIN.

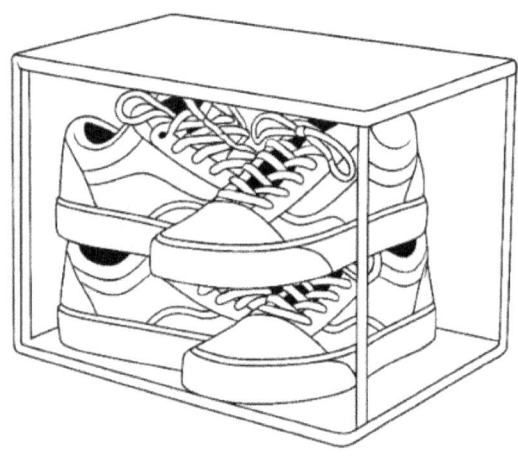

The right furniture and storage solutions can be game-changers for the ADHD brain. They can either support a functional, organized home or create more frustration. This chapter is about making intentional choices that work with your brain's natural tendencies, rather than against them. It's about viewing furniture not just for its aesthetic appeal, but as a tool for organization and a supportive element in your daily life.

The "Out of Sight, Out of Mind" Trap

Traditional storage often relies on putting things away in closed cabinets and drawers. For the ADHD brain, this can be a significant problem. If we can't see an item, we forget it exists. This phenomenon is directly tied to challenges with **working memory** and **object permanence**, core aspects of executive dysfunction. An item in a closed drawer is, for all intents and purposes, a forgotten item until a frantic, last-minute search ensues. This is where the balance between hidden and visible storage becomes a critical strategy.

- **Use Clear Containers:** Clear bins in your pantry, closet, and fridge make it easy to see what you have and where it is. This provides a crucial visual cue that bypasses the need for working memory. You no longer have to remember that the extra box of cereal is on the top shelf; you can see it. This makes it easier to find things and to know when you are running low on supplies.
- **Open Shelving:** For some, open shelving can be a great way to display items they need to remember, such as books, a watch collection, or daily-use kitchen items. This works best when the items are neatly arranged and serve a decorative purpose. By turning necessary items into a visual part of your home's aesthetic, you keep them in your line of sight without adding to visual clutter.

Functional Furniture: Your External Brain

When choosing furniture, think about its function for you, not just its aesthetic. The furniture in your home should act as an external brain, providing a clear, designated home for every item.

- **Landing Strips:** Use entry tables with drawers or a bench with built-in storage to create a functional "landing strip" for keys, mail, and other daily essentials. This is a physical, non-negotiable spot that catches items as they enter your home, preventing them from being scattered on every available surface. The presence of drawers or baskets provides an immediate, low-effort storage solution that reduces the mental energy required to put an item away.
- **Multi-Purpose Furniture:** Ottomans with hidden storage or beds with built-in drawers can be a great way to create extra storage without adding clutter to your space. A storage ottoman, for instance, can serve as a footrest, a coffee table,

and a tidy place to store blankets or magazines, all in one. This maximizes space and provides a simple, accessible home for items that would otherwise be left out.

The Power of Accessibility and Zones

The key to a successful storage system is accessibility. If it's difficult to put something away, the ADHD brain will, by default, choose the path of least resistance and leave it out.

- **Hooks vs. Hangers:** Consider the mental effort required. A hook requires one action: hang. A hanger requires multiple actions: open the closet door, find a hanger, put the garment on the hanger, and place it on the rod. For everyday items like coats and purses, a series of decorative hooks near the door is a far more functional and ADHD-friendly solution.

- **The "Zones" Method:** Think about your home in terms of functional "zones." For example, create a "paperwork zone" with a dedicated tray for incoming mail and a small filing box, a "keys and wallet zone" in your entryway, or a "reading zone" in your living room with a basket for books and magazines. This strategy reduces cognitive load by grouping similar items and tasks, which helps your brain locate and engage with what it needs more efficiently.

The goal is to design a home that is a supportive environment—a place where every item has a logical, accessible home that makes it easy for you to stay organized and find what you need. By being intentional with your furniture and storage choices, you're not just decorating your home; you're building a system that allows you to live with greater ease and less anxiety. This is an act of self-care and a foundational strategy for a more peaceful and productive life.

CHAPTER 6:

SENSORY-FRIENDLY CLEANING:
MAKING CHORES LESS OVERWHELMING

Why Cleaning Can Feel Like an Assault

If you've ever put off vacuuming because the noise made your teeth clench, or avoided scrubbing the bathroom because the smell of bleach made you gag, you're not alone. Many people with ADHD also experience heightened **sensory sensitivities**. That means sights, sounds, smells, textures, and even temperatures hit harder than they do for neurotypical people.

This is why cleaning, which already demands executive function skills, can feel doubly punishing. It's not just about remembering steps and following through, it's about enduring a barrage of sensory discomfort. The harsh squeak of a sponge, the chemical tang of cleaners, the scratch of dust against your throat, the sticky feeling of soap residue on your hands, it all stacks up into one overwhelming, unpleasant experience.

For some, it's not even about sensitivity but about **sensory boredom**. Cleaning feels unbearably dull, like your brain is deprived of stimulation and screaming for something else. Both overstimulation and understimulation can make cleaning feel like torture.

The good news? You can design cleaning routines that are **sensory-friendly**, ones that minimize overwhelm and even add comfort, stimulation, or pleasure to the process.

The ADHD–Sensory Connection

ADHD brains process sensory input differently. Some people are **sensory seekers**, craving more stimulation to stay engaged. Others are **sensory avoiders**, feeling overwhelmed by too much input. And many fluctuate between the two, depending on the day, task, or environment.

That means the exact same cleaning task can feel totally different from one person to the next:

- One person might find vacuuming soothing because it's loud and rhythmic.
- Another might find it unbearable, like nails on a chalkboard.
- One might enjoy the smell of lemon cleaner because it feels fresh and stimulating.
- Another might gag at the chemical scent and abandon the whole task.

Understanding your sensory profile is key. Instead of fighting against your brain, you can tailor cleaning to your comfort level, making it less punishing and more sustainable.

Step 1: Identify Your Sensory Triggers

The first step is noticing which parts of cleaning overwhelm or shut you down. Pay attention to the five senses:

- **Sight:** Clutter, bright lights, or visual chaos that makes your brain spiral.

- **Sound:** Loud vacuums, scraping chairs, or the buzz of appliances.
- **Smell:** Harsh cleaners, mildew, garbage odors.
- **Touch:** Sticky residues, slimy sponges, gritty dust, soggy rags.
- **Taste:** Less common, but some people are sensitive to chemical taste in the air.

Ask yourself: Which of these make me dread cleaning? Which are tolerable? Which are secretly enjoyable? Your answers will guide which hacks to adopt.

Step 2: Choose Sensory-Friendly Cleaning Tools

Sometimes the difference between dread and ease is simply using the right tools.

- **Noise Sensitivity:**
  - Use quieter vacuums (many stick vacuums are softer than old uprights).
  - Wear noise-canceling headphones or earplugs while vacuuming.
  - Turn cleaning into a sensory "bubble" by listening to upbeat music or podcasts.
- **Smell Sensitivity:**
  - Switch to unscented cleaners.
  - Use vinegar, baking soda, or mild soap instead of harsh chemicals.
  - Dilute concentrated cleaners more than the bottle suggests.
  - Open windows for fresh air.
- **Texture Sensitivity:**
  - Wear gloves (latex-free if needed) to avoid slimy or sticky textures.
  - Use microfiber cloths (soft, non-scratchy, quick-drying).
  - Replace steel wool or abrasive sponges with gentler scrubbers.

- **Visual Overload:**
  - Break large messes into smaller zones so you don't take in all the chaos at once.
  - Use bins or baskets to contain mess during cleaning so you see progress quickly.

It's not about being fancy. It's about **making cleaning tolerable** so you'll actually do it.

Step 3: Adjust the Environment

You don't have to accept your cleaning environment as-is. Small tweaks can completely change how it feels.

- **Lighting:** Harsh overhead lights can make dirt more visible but also feel oppressive. Try warm-toned bulbs or lamps.
- **Air Quality:** Run an air purifier while dusting, or use fans to move air while cleaning bathrooms.
- **Temperature:** If heat makes you cranky, set a cooler temperature before cleaning. If cold makes you avoid chores, cozy up with socks and a hoodie first.
- **Soundscape:** Create a playlist that energizes you, or listen to white noise to block out unpleasant sounds.

Think of cleaning less as a "task" and more as creating a **sensory setting** that supports your comfort.

Step 4: Add Pleasant Sensory Input

If cleaning is boring or uncomfortable, balance it with input that feels good.

- **Make it Musical:** Blast upbeat songs or calming instrumental tracks, depending on your mood.
- **Gamify It:** Set a timer with a fun sound, or challenge yourself to "beat the buzzer."
- **Scents You Love:** If strong smells overwhelm you, choose a gentle essential oil diffuser while you clean.
- **Movement Boosts:** Dance while sweeping, or stretch while folding laundry.

This doesn't erase the discomfort of certain chores, but it gives your brain positive stimulation to make the experience less punishing.

Step 5: Modify the Task Itself

Sometimes the best solution is to **do the task differently**. ADHD brains thrive when we adapt tasks instead of forcing rigid methods.

- **Vacuum Alternative:** If vacuuming noise is unbearable, use a broom or quiet handheld vacuum for small areas.
- **Dish Dread:** If slimy dishes are a sensory nightmare, rinse them immediately after use or run them through a quick soak before handling.
- **Bathroom Tasks:** Use disposable wipes instead of cloths if scrubbing textures bother you.
- **Dusting:** Use dusters with extendable handles so you don't feel particles on your skin.

Cleaning doesn't have to follow "the right way." It only has to follow **the way you'll actually do it**.

Step 6: Break It Into Micro-Tasks

Sensory overload often comes from trying to endure too much at once. Instead, shrink tasks into tolerable bites.

- Wipe one counter, not the whole kitchen.
- Vacuum one rug, not the whole floor.
- Do one load of laundry, not "all the laundry."

This keeps the sensory input brief and makes it easier to recover between steps.

Step 7: Build Recovery Into Your Routine

Even with hacks, cleaning can still be draining. Plan for **sensory recovery**:

- Rinse your hands with warm water after touching unpleasant textures.
- Step outside for fresh air after using cleaners.
- Take a quiet moment after vacuuming if the noise rattled you.

- Reward yourself with a pleasant sensory experience afterward (tea, a soft blanket, a scented candle you enjoy).

Recovery isn't indulgent, it's part of making the task sustainable.

Case Study 1: Kevin and the Vacuum

Kevin dreaded vacuuming. The roar of the machine made his heart race, and he'd avoid the task for weeks, letting crumbs pile up.

His solution? He bought a quieter stick vacuum, wore noise-canceling headphones, and set a 5-minute timer with his favorite song. He still didn't *love* vacuuming, but it went from intolerable to manageable. He vacuumed weekly instead of monthly, and his space felt lighter as a result.

Case Study 2: Dana and the Dishes

Dana hated doing dishes because the slimy food bits made her gag. She'd let dishes pile until the sink was a mountain.

Her fix: she wore thick dish gloves, added a drop of lemon essential oil to her soap for a pleasant scent, and rinsed dishes immediately after meals to avoid buildup. Suddenly, dishes were no longer torture—they were just part of her routine.

Step 8: Shift From Punishment to Care

For many of us, cleaning feels tied to shame. Maybe you were scolded as a child for not doing chores "right." Maybe you've internalized the idea that a clean house equals moral worth. When you combine shame with sensory overwhelm, no wonder cleaning feels like punishment.

Reframe cleaning as **self-care, not self-punishment**.

- Wiping your counters isn't a chore, it's giving Future You a fresh start.
- Vacuuming isn't torture, it's creating a calmer sensory environment.
- Washing dishes isn't punishment, it's setting up tomorrow's meals with ease.

When you change the narrative, cleaning feels less like suffering and more like kindness.

Step 9: Accept "Good Enough"

Sensory-friendly cleaning is not about spotless perfection. It's about creating a livable space without overwhelming your senses.

If you only wipe half the counter today, that's still better than none. If you vacuum just the high-traffic areas, that's still progress.

ADHD thrives on **permission to be imperfect**. When you accept "good enough," you reduce pressure and make cleaning a task you can return to instead of avoid.

Step 10: Layer Sensory Strategies Together

One hack helps. Three or four together? That's when cleaning becomes sustainable.

Example: Cleaning the bathroom might mean...

- Wearing gloves for textures.
- Opening a window for airflow.
- Playing upbeat music.
- Using mild, unscented cleaners.
- Taking a shower afterward as recovery.

Each layer softens the sensory impact until the task is doable.

Closing Thought

For ADHD brains, cleaning often feels like punishment because it bombards us with sensory input we didn't choose. But you don't have to endure cleaning the way others expect you to. You can adapt it to your needs, softening, customizing, and reframing until it's no longer torture.

A sensory-friendly approach isn't about luxury. It's about practicality. It's about recognizing that your brain and body deserve systems that work *for you*, not against you.

When you reduce sensory overwhelm and add sensory comfort, cleaning stops being an assault and starts being... tolerable. Maybe even enjoyable. And that small shift makes all the difference in creating a home where you can thrive.

CHAPTER 7:

CLEANING IN MOTION:
TURNING TASKS INTO MOVEMENT BREAKS

Why Cleaning Feels Like a Chore

For most people with ADHD, the hardest part about cleaning isn't the cleaning itself, it's getting started. Sitting still and telling yourself, *"Okay, I have to spend the next three hours scrubbing this house"* is overwhelming before you even pick up a sponge. It feels heavy, boring, and endless.

But here's something important: ADHD brains **love movement**. We crave stimulation. We think more clearly when our bodies are engaged. That's why pacing while talking on the phone feels natural, or why ideas pop into your head when you're walking instead of sitting at your desk.

Movement helps regulate dopamine, and dopamine is exactly what's missing when a cleaning task feels impossible.

So what if cleaning wasn't a dreaded block of time, but instead a **series of movement breaks**? What if instead of punishment, cleaning became energy? That's the mindset shift behind "Cleaning in Motion."

The ADHD Brain and Movement

Science has shown that physical activity boosts dopamine and norepinephrine—the very neurotransmitters ADHD brains struggle to regulate. This is why exercise often makes ADHD symptoms feel lighter: focus improves, moods stabilize, and tasks feel more manageable afterward.

Cleaning isn't always thought of as exercise, but many chores qualify as **functional movement**: squatting, reaching, lifting, walking, bending, twisting. The difference is perspective. Instead of seeing chores as something to suffer through, reframing them as opportunities for natural movement can make them more engaging, stimulating, and sustainable.

Step 1: Redefine Cleaning as "Micro-Workouts"

You don't need a treadmill or a gym membership to move your body. Every time you sweep, scrub, or vacuum, you're already doing physical work. The trick is to start noticing, and celebrating, that movement.

- **Vacuuming:** Walking lunges with extra resistance.
- **Wiping counters:** Shoulder and arm workout.
- **Laundry:** Squats from lifting baskets, stretching while folding.
- **Sweeping or mopping:** Core twists and rhythmic cardio.
- **Decluttering:** Carrying items back and forth like weighted steps.

Instead of groaning about having to clean, think: *I'm sneaking in a few minutes of movement that my body and brain will thank me for.*

Step 2: Use Music and Rhythm

Movement becomes easier when it has rhythm. That's why people walk faster to upbeat songs or naturally match their pace to a beat. Music transforms chores into dance.

- Make a playlist with 3–5 high-energy songs. Each track is one "cleaning sprint."
- Match your actions to the beat: wipe to the rhythm, sweep in time, fold clothes on the downbeat.
- Rotate playlists so novelty keeps you engaged.

This approach does two things:

1. It makes cleaning fun instead of flat.
2. It keeps time limited, three songs equals about 10 minutes, which is a manageable micro-cleaning session.

Step 3: Turn Cleaning Into Movement Breaks

Long cleaning marathons are overwhelming. Short bursts feel doable. Instead of "cleaning the kitchen," try:

- Wiping counters for 2 minutes between emails.
- Vacuuming one rug after a phone call.
- Folding laundry during a podcast break.

By reframing chores as **movement breaks**, you satisfy your body's craving for stimulation and avoid the ADHD trap of endless sitting.

Step 4: Gamify the Experience

ADHD brains thrive on novelty, challenge, and reward. Turning cleaning into a game provides that dopamine hit.

- **Beat the Timer:** Can you unload the dishwasher before the song ends?
- **Zone Cleaning:** Race against yourself to see how fast you can reset one area.
- **Step Counter Challenge:** Track steps while cleaning, see how many you rack up.

- **Family Game:** Assign everyone a zone and play "cleaning relay."

Games add playfulness and stimulation, which shifts cleaning from obligation to challenge.

Step 5: Stack Cleaning With Other Stimulation

If cleaning feels too boring, pair it with something else stimulating. This turns cleaning into background movement rather than the sole focus.

- Listen to an audiobook, podcast, or comedy show.
- Call a friend while tidying.
- Watch a TV show while folding laundry.
- Use body doubling, clean on video chat with someone else.

The cleaning becomes secondary to the enjoyable activity, which tricks your brain into getting it done.

Step 6: Break Cleaning Into "Circuits"

Think of your home as a workout circuit. Instead of slogging through one task for an hour, rotate through small sets of chores.

Example circuit:

1. Wipe counters (2 minutes).
2. Sweep kitchen floor (2 minutes).
3. Put laundry in the washer (2 minutes).
4. Declutter the entryway (2 minutes).

Repeat the circuit once or twice, and you'll have tackled multiple zones without burning out. Circuits keep variety high and boredom low, perfect for ADHD brains.

Step 7: Use Movement to Manage Energy

Some days you're buzzing with restlessness. Others, you feel like a slug. Cleaning can meet you where you are.

- **On hyperactive days:** Channel restless energy into high-motion tasks (vacuuming, scrubbing floors, hauling laundry).

- **On low-energy days:** Choose gentler tasks (dusting, folding clothes, wiping mirrors).

The key is to let your body guide which cleaning tasks fit your energy level, rather than forcing a rigid plan.

Step 8: Build "Anchor Routines"

Anchor routines pair a movement with a chore so it becomes automatic.

- After brushing your teeth, wipe the bathroom counter.
- While waiting for your coffee, unload the dishwasher.
- During TV commercials, fold a few pieces of laundry.

Over time, these micro-movements become habitual, like brushing your teeth itself. They're no longer chores, just natural extensions of your day.

Step 9: Celebrate Progress Visibly

One of the best motivators for ADHD brains is **seeing immediate results**. Cleaning in motion offers lots of visual wins: a cleared counter, a vacuumed rug, a tidy shelf.

Instead of focusing on the long road ahead, pause to notice the visible difference you made in just a few minutes of movement. The brain gets a dopamine boost, which fuels motivation to keep going later.

Step 10: Reframe Cleaning as Self-Expression

Here's the deeper shift: Cleaning doesn't have to feel like punishment. It can be a form of self-expression and empowerment.

- Dancing while mopping turns drudgery into performance.
- Choosing tools and products you like (a colorful broom, a lavender-scented spray) makes the process more personal.
- Moving your body with rhythm and intention turns "chores" into an embodied practice of care.

This isn't about pretending cleaning is glamorous, it's about claiming it as something that works *for you* rather than against you.

Case Study 1: Nadia and the Afternoon Slump

Nadia worked from home and hit a wall around 3 PM daily. She'd scroll on her phone, groggy and unproductive. One day, instead of fighting the slump, she tried a 10-minute "cleaning sprint." She blasted two upbeat songs, danced around while sweeping, and wiped the counters. By the time she sat back down, she was energized, and her kitchen was cleaner. Cleaning became her daily "reset ritual" instead of wasted time.

Case Study 2: James and the Family Game

James dreaded family cleaning days. His kids complained, and he'd feel frustrated when nothing got done. He decided to gamify it: each family member had a zone, and they raced to finish before a 15-minute playlist ended. They'd blast music and laugh at each other's goofy dance moves. Suddenly, cleaning wasn't a fight, it was bonding. The house wasn't spotless, but it was livable, and the family enjoyed the process.

Step 11: Lower the Bar to Keep Moving

The trap of perfection kills momentum. If you think, *I need to deep-clean the entire kitchen,* your brain freezes. But if you think, *I'll just dance-wipe this counter for two minutes,* you're more likely to start.

Small motion leads to bigger motion. Once you're moving, you might keep going. But even if you don't, you've already made progress.

Step 12: Link Cleaning to Joyful Movement

If cleaning is dull, link it with movements you *do* enjoy:

- Dance while folding laundry.
- Do squats while picking things off the floor.
- Stretch while wiping windows.
- Put on roller skates to sweep a large room.

Silly? Maybe. Effective? Absolutely. ADHD thrives on novelty and fun, why not make cleaning part of it?

Step 13: Use Cleaning as Transition Rituals

ADHD brains struggle with transitions, switching from one task to another feels jarring. Cleaning in motion can act as a bridge.

- Do a 5-minute cleaning sprint between work and dinner.
- Wipe down a table between study sessions.
- Vacuum one room before moving into relaxation mode.

These rituals mark the end of one activity and prepare your brain for the next.

Step 14: Track Motion, Not Perfection

Instead of tracking spotless rooms, track movement. Did you do 15 minutes of cleaning sprints today? Great. Did you rack up 2,000 steps while decluttering? Amazing.

When you measure motion instead of perfection, cleaning feels less like judgment and more like progress.

Step 15: Create Movement Zones

Design your home with "movement-friendly" cleaning in mind:

- Keep lightweight tools accessible (hand vac, dusting wand).
- Store cleaning supplies in each room to reduce barriers.
- Place baskets where clutter collects so you can tidy with a single movement.

When tools are easy to grab, it's easier to turn small bursts of energy into quick cleaning motions.

Step 16: Respect Your Body's Limits

While cleaning can be reframed as movement, it's not about pushing yourself into exhaustion. ADHD brains often forget to notice physical fatigue until it's too late.

- Pace yourself with short bursts.
- Use ergonomic tools (lightweight vacuums, long-handled dusters).
- Listen to your body, stop before you hit sensory or physical burnout.

Sustainability matters more than intensity.

Closing Thought

Cleaning doesn't have to be a punishment. For ADHD brains, it can be **stimulation, movement, energy, and even joy**. When you reframe chores as opportunities to move, dance, stretch, and reset, you free yourself from the heavy, shame-filled narrative that cleaning must be endless drudgery.

Your home doesn't need perfection, it needs motion. A few steps, a few wipes, a few bursts of energy, that's enough to keep the cycle going. Cleaning in motion is about shifting from stillness and overwhelm into action and rhythm. And once you see it this way, chores stop being punishment and start being part of the vibrant, kinetic life your ADHD brain was built for.

Reflection Questions:

- *Book 3 offered several strategies for tackling clutter in specific areas, such as the kitchen, closets, and paperwork. Which of these "chaos hotspots" in your own home feels the most overwhelming to you, and what is one small, manageable change you can make this week to begin a "Keep, Toss, Donate" session?*

- *We also discussed the "One-In, One-Out" rule and the importance of functional furniture. Reflect on your last few purchases. Was there an item you bought on impulse that could have been handled differently? What is one way you could apply the "One-In, One-Out" rule to a future purchase?*

- *Think about the concept of **"cognitive load"**. Which piece of furniture or storage in your home is not currently working for you, and what small change could you make to a piece of furniture or storage solution to reduce the mental energy you spend on that space?*

- *The **"Keep, Toss, Donate"** method encourages quick decisions. What is one item you've been putting off making a decision about, and what is the one-sentence justification you can use to either keep it, toss it, or donate it?*

- What is one **"chaos hotspot"** that you feel a sense of shame about? How can you reframe that space from a "mess" to an "opportunity" to create a system that works for your brain, rather than against it?

BOOK FOUR:

THE CLEANING TOOLKIT AND TIME MANAGEMENT

CHAPTER 1:

THE ADHD-FRIENDLY CLEANING KIT: ONLY THE ESSENTIALS YOU'LL ACTUALLY USE.

For many people, a trip down the cleaning aisle can be overwhelming. The sheer number of products, each promising a specific, miraculous result, can lead to **decision fatigue** and clutter. For the ADHD brain, a complicated toolkit is a barrier to starting. The mental effort required to decide which product to use for which surface, or where to even find the right tool, can be enough to trigger task paralysis. This chapter is about simplifying your cleaning supplies to the essentials, making the process less daunting and more practical.

The goal isn't to be a minimalist cleaning guru; it's to create a low-friction system that removes the mental roadblocks that prevent you from starting a cleaning task in the first place.

The "Less Is More" Approach

You don't need a different product for every surface. A simple, effective cleaning kit can be built with just a few key items. The neuro-psychological benefit of this approach is that it significantly reduces **cognitive load**. When you have one product for most jobs, you eliminate the micro-decision of "Which cleaner should I use?" and can get straight to the task.

The foundational kit includes:

- **All-Purpose Cleaner:** A good all-purpose cleaner can handle most surfaces in your kitchen and bathroom. Look for one that is non-toxic and multi-surface. These cleaners use a combination of **surfactants**, molecules that reduce the surface tension of water, and mild solvents to lift dirt, grease, and grime from surfaces. This single product can effectively replace separate countertop sprays, floor cleaners, and bathroom sprays, thereby drastically reducing the visual clutter under your sink.

- **Microfiber Cloths:** These are highly effective for dusting and wiping without leaving streaks. The magic of microfiber lies in its composition: it's made of tiny synthetic fibers that are split into microscopic hooks and loops. These fibers create a greater surface area and a positive electrostatic charge that attracts and holds onto dirt and dust. Having a separate color for different rooms (e.g., blue for the bathroom, green for the kitchen) can help with **cross-contamination** and keep things organized. This simple **color-coding system** is another external brain strategy that helps you avoid mental mistakes and ensures you're not using the same cloth for your toilet and your kitchen counter.

- **A Solid Vacuum or Broom:** A tool you can easily grab and use is key. Consider a cordless vacuum for quick, low-friction cleanups. For the ADHD brain, the effort of dragging out a heavy, corded vacuum is often a significant barrier to action. A lightweight, cordless option can be a game-changer, making a quick ten-minute vacuum feel less like a chore and more like a simple, spontaneous act.

- **Glass Cleaner:** For windows and mirrors. While an all-purpose cleaner can often work on glass, a dedicated glass cleaner is one of the few exceptions worth making, as it is specifically formulated to dry quickly and leave no streaks, ensuring a visually calm, satisfying result.
- **Toilet Cleaner and Brush:** A dedicated set for the bathroom is essential for hygiene and should be kept within easy reach of the toilet.
- **Rubber Gloves:** Essential for protecting your hands during deep cleaning, a small but important act of self-care.

By keeping your supplies minimal and accessible, you're reducing the mental hurdle of "Where do I even start?" Your cleaning kit should be a supportive tool, not another source of clutter and overwhelm.

The Cleaning Caddy: Your Portable Command Center

Having a minimal list of supplies is only half the battle; the other half is making them accessible. This is where the **cleaning caddy** comes in. A caddy is a small, portable container, a bucket, a large basket, or a divided box, that holds all your essential cleaning supplies in one place.

The genius of the cleaning caddy is that it completely eliminates the need to hunt for supplies. Instead of wandering from room to room, gathering cloths, sprays, and brushes, you simply grab your caddy, and everything you need is right there. This dramatically lowers the **activation barrier**, the mental effort required to start a task. The caddy transforms a multi-step process ("find the supplies, then clean") into a single-step one ("grab the caddy, then clean").

Your cleaning caddy should contain:

- Your all-purpose cleaner
- Your glass cleaner
- A set of your color-coded microfiber cloths
- A small brush for scrubbing
- Your rubber gloves

Keep this caddy in a central location, like under the kitchen sink, so it's always ready to go. When you need to do a five-minute tidy or a ten-minute sprint, the caddy becomes your portable "command center," allowing you to move quickly and efficiently from one task to the next without losing momentum.

The Power of Scent and Sound

Cleaning is often a monotonous task, and monotony is the Achilles' heel of the ADHD brain. It craves novelty and stimulation, and when a task is repetitive and uninteresting, the brain will seek a dopamine hit elsewhere, leading to distraction. This is where you can intentionally introduce sensory input to make cleaning more engaging.

- **Scent:** The smell of a clean space is a powerful reward in itself, but you can also use scent as a motivator. Choose an all-purpose cleaner with a scent you enjoy. This small sensory detail can make the task more pleasant. You can also use an essential oil diffuser with scents like peppermint or citrus, which have been shown to improve focus and energy.

- **Sound:** Music or a podcast can act as a form of **auditory scaffolding** for the ADHD brain. A good playlist can help you maintain focus by providing a consistent external rhythm that overrides the internal mental chatter. It turns a tedious chore into a small, personal party. Podcasts or audiobooks can also serve this purpose, providing a narrative to follow while your body is engaged in a repetitive task. Just be mindful of your choices: if a podcast is too engaging, it can become a distraction.

Putting It All Together: A Low-Friction Cleaning System

Your essential cleaning supply list is the foundation, but a true system is what makes it work. By keeping your supplies minimal and organizing them in a cleaning caddy, you are creating a system that is easy to start and easy to maintain. By adding sensory elements like music or a pleasant scent, you are making the task more enjoyable and supportive of your brain's natural tendencies. This isn't about fighting your brain; it's about working with it. You are designing a system that respects your energy levels, rewards your efforts, and makes a clean, organized home an achievable and sustainable reality.

CHAPTER 2:

TIME-BLOCKING MADE SIMPLE: SCHEDULING HACKS THAT KEEP YOU ON TRACK WITHOUT STRESS.

Time blindness is a common challenge for those with ADHD. It's not a character flaw or a sign of being lazy; it's a neurobiological reality. The ADHD brain often struggles to accurately perceive the passage of time, making it difficult to estimate how long a task will take. This is rooted in a dysfunction of the brain's executive functions, particularly in the prefrontal cortex, which is responsible for temporal reasoning and planning. Tasks that we think will take ten minutes can stretch into hours, and major projects can seem impossible to start because we can't mentally map out the steps. This chapter introduces simple, ADHD-friendly scheduling hacks that help you manage your time effectively without rigid, unrealistic rules.

The purpose of these strategies is to create an **external brain**, a system of cues and structures that compensates for an internal sense of time that is often unreliable.

Time-Blocking with a Twist

Time-blocking is the practice of scheduling specific blocks of time for certain tasks. For the ADHD brain, a full hour of "clean the kitchen" is often a non-starter. It feels vague, overwhelming, and doesn't provide a clear finish line. A flexible, ADHD-friendly approach is needed.

Focus Sprints: The Power of the Pomodoro

Instead of blocking off a full hour, try using **Focus Sprints**. Block off 20-30 minute "sprints" of focused work, followed by a 10-15 minute break. This is a direct application of the **Pomodoro Technique**, a time-management method that has been proven to be highly effective for those with ADHD. The neuroscientific reason this works is twofold:

1. **Reduced Activation Barrier:** A 20-minute task is far less intimidating than a two-hour task. The short duration lowers the mental hurdle to get started, making it easier to overcome procrastination.

2. **Built-In Dopamine:** The built-in break provides a crucial reward. Completing a sprint and taking a break gives your brain a small, immediate dopamine hit, which reinforces the positive behavior and makes you more likely to start the next sprint. This prevents the burnout that comes from trying to maintain prolonged focus.

These breaks are not just a reward; they are an essential part of the process. They allow your mind to wander, to seek the novelty it craves, and to recharge. Sometimes, a sprint can lead you into a state of **hyperfocus** or **"flow,"** where you become so engrossed that you lose track of time. In these moments, it's fine to extend the sprint, but be mindful of a crash afterward. The sprints are a safety net that allows you to work intensely without the fear of getting stuck or burning out.

Task Batching: Reducing Mental Switching Costs

The ADHD brain expends a significant amount of mental energy when it has to switch from one type of task to another. This is known as **"mental switching cost."** The act of putting away dishes, then remembering to pay a bill, then trying to write an email, is a cognitive tax that drains your energy.

Task Batching is a strategy that groups similar tasks together. For example, instead of doing one chore at a time, batch all your "quick tidy" tasks (e.g., wiping counters, putting away clothes, tidying the living room) into one 20-minute sprint. This allows your brain to stay in a single "mode" and conserve precious mental energy. You'll find that you can complete a lot more in a shorter amount of time because you're not constantly fighting against the friction of changing tasks. Other examples include:

- **"Phone Call Batching":** Make all your necessary phone calls (doctor's appointments, customer service) in one block.
- **"Email Batching":** Check and respond to emails only at specific times, like at the start and end of your day.
- **"Errand Batching":** Plan your errands to be in the same geographic area to minimize travel time and mental fatigue.

The Power of the Timer

A timer is one of the most powerful tools in your toolkit. It's a non-judgmental, external cue that helps you stay aware of the passage of time without constant mental effort. It serves as your external brain, helping with both task initiation and task completion.

- **To Get Started:** The timer removes the need for you to "feel" motivated. The simple act of setting a timer for 20 minutes and saying, "I just have to work on this until the timer dings," is often enough to overcome the initial hurdle of starting.
- **To Stay on Track:** The timer provides a constant, external reminder that prevents you from getting lost in a **hyperfocus** loop or a distracting detour.

- **To Stop:** The timer also gives you permission to stop. When the timer goes off, you can walk away with a sense of accomplishment, regardless of how much you've completed. This prevents burnout and reinforces the idea that progress, not perfection, is the goal.

There are many types of timers, each with its own benefits. A simple kitchen timer can work, but for a visual reminder of time, a **visual timer** that shows the time ticking down (like a disappearing colored wedge) can be incredibly effective.

Additional Scheduling Hacks

The "Start-Stop" Method

Instead of just scheduling a task, schedule the **start** and **stop** of it. For example, your calendar entry shouldn't just say "work on report." It should say, "10:00 AM - Start report" and "10:30 AM - Stop report." This makes the task feel finite and less daunting. The explicit "stop" time gives you permission to walk away, which is crucial for a brain that struggles with completion and can feel overwhelmed by an open-ended task.

Body Doubling

Body doubling is the practice of working on a task in the presence of another person, even if they aren't helping. The presence of another person provides a subtle form of accountability and an external anchor for your focus. This is a powerful psychological tool that can help you with task initiation and follow-through. A "body double" could be a friend working in the same room, a partner doing their own chores, or even a virtual "co-working" session with someone on a video call. The social element provides a gentle pressure that can help override procrastination.

The "Parking Lot" or "Distraction Pad"

Distracting thoughts are a normal part of the ADHD brain. During a focus sprint, an unrelated idea or a forgotten task will almost inevitably pop into your head. Instead of following the thought and derailing your current task, use a **"parking lot"** or **"distraction pad."** This is a simple piece of paper or a notes app where you immediately jot down the distracting thought. You are acknowledging the thought, but you are not acting on it. This allows your brain to let go of the thought without the fear of forgetting it, freeing up your mental resources to return to the task at hand.

The Power of Transition

The ADHD brain can find it difficult to switch from one task to another. To make this easier, build in a small, ritualistic action to signal the end of one task and the beginning of the next. This could be a five-minute stretch, making a cup of tea, or a short walk. These **micro-breaks** help the brain reset and create a clear mental boundary between tasks, making the transition smoother and less jarring.

The Role of a "Buffer Zone"

Never schedule tasks back-to-back. Leave 10-15 minute **"buffer zones"** between each scheduled task. This accounts for the unpredictable nature of ADHD time perception and the inevitable delays that occur in daily life. A buffer zone reduces the stress of being late or behind schedule and provides a much-needed moment of breathing room.

By combining these hacks, you can create a robust external system that supports your internal challenges. The goal isn't to be perfect, but to be intentional. You are moving from a feeling of being a victim of time to being an active, intentional manager of it.

CHAPTER 3:

MAKE IT FUN OR IT WON'T GET DONE: TURNING CHORES INTO GAMES YOU'LL ACTUALLY PLAY.

The ADHD brain is driven by interest, novelty, and challenge. Monotonous tasks like cleaning are often boring, which makes them incredibly difficult to start and finish. The reason for this is rooted in neurobiology: our brains use a neurotransmitter called **dopamine** to regulate motivation, attention, and reward. Repetitive, low-stimulus tasks like washing dishes or folding laundry produce very little dopamine, so the ADHD brain, which already struggles with dopamine regulation, finds it hard to engage. This is why a simple chore can feel like a monumental, impossible task.

This chapter is about turning boring chores into engaging "games" that hack your brain's reward system and make organization and cleaning feel less like a chore and more like a game. These strategies aren't tricks to fool yourself; they are intentional, neurobiologically-informed approaches to make tasks more appealing by introducing the very elements your brain craves: a clear goal, a sense of urgency, and a tangible reward.

Turning Tasks into Games: Hacking Your Reward System

The key to a successful cleaning game is to pair a low-dopamine task (the chore) with a high-dopamine activity (the game or the reward). This is a process known as **dopamine stacking**, and it's a powerful tool for building habits and overcoming procrastination.

The "Beat the Clock" Game

Set a timer for a short, challenging amount of time (e.g., 5-15 minutes) and see how much you can get done. The time limit creates a sense of urgency and turns a simple task into a race. This works by tapping into your brain's natural desire for a challenge. The clock isn't an enemy; it's a friendly competitor. You're not racing against time, you're racing against your own personal best. This simple act of time-boxing gives the task a clear start and end point, which is crucial for a brain with **time blindness**. The timer becomes an external cue that keeps you focused and prevents you from getting lost in a task that has no clear end. When the timer dings, you can stop, regardless of whether the task is completely finished, and still feel a sense of accomplishment.

This game can be applied to almost any chore:

- "How many dishes can I put away in five minutes?"
- "Can I vacuum the living room in ten minutes?"
- "Can I clear the kitchen counter in three minutes?"

The "Podcast/Music" Game

Only allow yourself to listen to your favorite podcast or music when you are doing a specific chore. This is a classic example of dopamine stacking. You are linking a low-interest activity with a high-interest one. By making your entertainment contingent on your chore, you create a powerful incentive to get started. You can take this a step further by having a specific playlist or podcast that is reserved only for cleaning. This creates a ritual and a mental cue: when the "cleaning playlist" comes on, your brain knows it's time to get to work. The music provides a consistent rhythm and stimulation that helps to override the monotony of the task.

The "Reward System"

Create a simple reward for yourself after you finish a chore. The key to a successful reward system is that the reward must be **immediate, tangible, and not so large that it becomes a distraction.** A delayed or abstract reward is often not enough to motivate the ADHD brain.

- **Small, Immediate Rewards:** 5 minutes of phone time, a square of chocolate, a new episode of your favorite 15-minute show, or a moment of relaxation with a cup of tea.
- **The "Trophy Room" Game:** Create a visible reward system. After completing a chore, you get to place something (a sticker, a checkmark on a list, or a "trophy" item) in a visible spot. This externalizes the reward and provides a powerful visual record of your progress, which is incredibly motivating.

The "One-Song Tidy"

Pick one of your favorite songs and clean for its duration. The length of the song provides a natural time boundary, and the music makes the task more enjoyable. This is a great, low-commitment way to start. It's a non-intimidating way to get started and get a small win. The simplicity of this game is its greatest strength.

Advanced Gamification: Turning Chores into Engaging Projects

Once you've mastered the basics, you can move on to more advanced ways of gamifying chores, which tap into different aspects of the ADHD brain's needs.

The "Co-op Cleaning" Game

For the ADHD brain, social interaction and accountability are powerful motivators. The concept of **body doubling** is a cornerstone of this strategy. You can invite a friend or family member to help you clean, or even just have them on a video call while you both do chores in your respective homes. The presence of another person provides a subtle form of accountability and an external anchor for your focus. It turns a solitary, boring task into a shared, social experience. You're no longer alone with your thoughts; you're part of a team, and the shared experience makes the time pass more quickly and enjoyably.

The "Deep Dive Challenge"

Connect this to the concept of **hyperfocus**. Instead of dreading a tedious task, turn it into a deep-focus project. This works best with a chore that has a clear end point and allows for a sense of mastery. For example:

- **"The Closet Overhaul":** Can you categorize and organize your entire closet in a series of timed sprints? The challenge and the clear goal make the task more appealing.
- **"The Pantry Pro":** See if you can organize your pantry to look like a professional grocery store aisle. This uses visual interest and a sense of creative challenge to engage your brain.

The "Task Bingo" or "Randomizer"

Monotony is the enemy of the ADHD brain. To combat this, use a simple randomizer to pick which chore to do next. Create a list of small chores and use a simple app or a bingo card to pick one. This introduces an element of **novelty and unpredictability**, which the brain finds highly engaging. It breaks the monotony of a fixed routine and makes the process of doing chores feel less like a repetitive obligation and more like a playful surprise.

The "Power of Transformation"

The ADHD brain is highly visual. You can use this to your advantage by framing cleaning as an act of **transformation**. Before you start a chore, take a picture of a messy space. After you've cleaned it, take another picture. The visual contrast is a powerful, dopamine-releasing reward. You have tangible proof of your effort and a clear record of your accomplishment. This visual reward is often more impactful than a simple mental acknowledgment and can be used to motivate you for future projects.

The Final Philosophy: Working with Your Brain, Not Against It

The goal of all these games and strategies is not to trick your brain, but to work with it. You are respecting your brain's need for novelty, urgency, and reward, and you are building a system that is supportive rather than restrictive. By reframing chores as games, you are changing your mindset from one of dread to one of possibility. You are building a sustainable system that allows you to live in a clean and organized home, not through willpower and grit, but through clever, intentional strategies that align with your unique neurodiversity. The end result is a cleaner home and a less stressed mind, and that is a win worth playing for.

CHAPTER 4:

DELEGATE, AUTOMATE, OUTSOURCE: CLEANING STRATEGIES WHEN YOU CAN'T DO IT ALL.

The myth that you have to do everything yourself is a major source of burnout and frustration, especially for individuals with ADHD. The human brain, regardless of neurotype, has a limited capacity for executive functions, the mental skills that include planning, organizing, and managing tasks. For those with ADHD, this capacity is often more easily depleted. Trying to manage every single task, from paying bills to doing laundry to cleaning the entire house, is a recipe for overwhelm. This chapter is about recognizing that it's okay to ask for help, and that delegating, automating, and outsourcing are not signs of failure; they are strategic choices for success and for creating a more sustainable, peaceful life. These strategies are proactive ways to conserve your limited mental energy and redirect it toward what you do best and what you genuinely enjoy.

Delegating with a Purpose: The Shared Mental Load

If you live with a partner, family, or roommates, delegation is key. The issue is not just about getting help; it's about addressing the **shared mental load** of running a household. The mental load refers to all the invisible labor involved in managing a household: the planning, the remembering, and the organizing of tasks. For a neurodiverse person, this can be an enormous, unseen source of stress.

Instead of simply asking for help, which can often lead to frustration and miscommunication, create a clear, shared system. The goal is to move from a place of unspoken assumptions to a system of clear, explicit agreements.

- **Use a Whiteboard or a Shared App:** A whiteboard in a central location, a shared to-do list app like Trello or Asana, or even a simple calendar can act as your external brain. This system provides a single source of truth for all household tasks. It externalizes the mental load, so you don't have to be the one constantly remembering who needs to do what.

- **Be Specific About What "Done" Means:** Avoid vague requests like "clean the kitchen." Instead, be specific. "Wipe down the counters, wash all the dishes in the sink, and sweep the floor." This removes ambiguity and reduces the likelihood of misunderstandings. The ADHD brain thrives on clear instructions and defined end points.

- **Play to Your Strengths:** Delegate tasks based on interest and skill. If your partner enjoys cooking but you hate doing dishes, make a deal. If you're great at organizing the pantry but they prefer taking out the trash, that's a win-win. This approach makes the tasks feel less like a chore and more like a contribution to the household team.

By delegating with a purpose, you're sharing the mental load, which is a powerful act of self-care and a cornerstone of a healthy shared living space.

Automating for Simplicity: The Set-and-Forget Strategy

Automation is a powerful tool for the ADHD brain. It's the ultimate "set-and-forget" strategy that removes the need for a decision, a reminder, or a mental effort. Every automated task is a small victory over the chaos of daily life. The neurobiological benefit is that you are essentially offloading a routine task from your brain's already strained executive functions to a reliable, external system.

- **Automatic Bill Pay:** Automate as many of your bills as possible to prevent late fees and anxiety. A forgotten bill is a classic consequence of time blindness and can be a major source of stress. By setting up automatic payments, you are completely removing the task from your mental to-do list. The effort to set it up once is far less than the cumulative effort and anxiety of remembering to pay every bill every month.

- **Subscription Boxes:** Use subscription services for things like meal kits, cleaning supplies, or even groceries. This reduces the mental effort of planning, shopping, and decision-making. Meal kits, for example, solve the triple problem of "what to cook," "what to buy," and "how to prepare it." This is a perfect example of a system that works with the ADHD brain, providing novelty and variety without the overwhelming effort of planning.

- **Automated Calendar Reminders:** Use your phone's calendar app to set up recurring reminders for chores like taking out the trash or watering plants. These are tasks that are easy to forget but have a significant impact when they're not done. A simple, recurring alert that says "Take out the trash" is an invaluable external cue that prevents you from having to rely on your unreliable working memory.

Outsourcing for Peace of Mind: A Strategic Investment

The idea of outsourcing certain tasks can feel like a luxury, but it's more accurately a **strategic investment in your mental health and well-being**. If a task consistently causes you stress, anxiety, or burnout, and you have the means, consider outsourcing it. The mental space you gain from outsourcing a task is often more valuable than the money you spend on it.

- **A Cleaning Service:** If cleaning your home consistently feels overwhelming and you have the financial means, hiring a cleaning service, even for just a few hours a month, can be a game-changer. The mental relief of knowing a major task is being handled is immense. It allows you to focus on the things you enjoy and reduces the shame and guilt that can accompany a messy home.

- **A Laundry Service:** For some, laundry is a multi-step, overwhelming task that is never truly finished. Outsourcing this to a service that handles washing, drying, and folding can be a profound source of peace.

- **A Virtual Assistant (VA):** For managing your digital life—organizing your email, scheduling appointments, or managing your digital files—a VA can be an invaluable tool. This is a perfect example of outsourcing a task that requires a high level of executive function and consistent attention, which are areas where the ADHD brain can struggle.

By delegating, automating, and outsourcing, you're creating a support system that frees up your energy for the things that you are uniquely good at and that bring you joy. You are not failing by asking for help; you are succeeding by building a sustainable system that allows you to thrive. You are making an intentional choice to live a life with less friction and more peace. This is the ultimate goal of organization: not to create a perfect home, but to create a life that feels more manageable, more joyful, and more authentically your own.

CHAPTER 5:

APPS THAT KEEP YOU MOVING: DIGITAL TOOLS TO SIMPLIFY YOUR ROUTINES AND REMINDERS.

Technology can be both a blessing and a curse for the ADHD brain. While a phone can be a source of endless distraction, a portal to social media scrolls and impulsive online shopping, it can also be a powerful tool for managing your life. This chapter explores how to use apps and technology to create a supportive, external system that helps you stay on track. The goal is to turn a potential source of chaos into a reliable **"digital scaffold,"** a framework that supports your daily life and compensates for the internal challenges of memory, attention, and time management.

The key to using technology effectively is to be intentional. Don't let your technology become another source of clutter and overwhelm. When used strategically, technology can be a powerful ally in building an organized and less chaotic life.

Your External Brain for Your Internal Thoughts

For the ADHD brain, which struggles with working memory, a simple thought can be a fleeting ghost that vanishes before you can act on it. A phone can act as a powerful "external brain" for all the things you need to remember. This is the digital version of a **brain dump**—a reliable, always-on system for capturing your mental fragments so your internal brain is free to focus on the task at hand.

To-Do List Apps: From Chaos to Clarity

To-do list apps are far more than just digital sticky notes. They are a place to capture all the tasks from your "brain dump" and organize them into manageable, actionable lists. The power of these apps lies in their ability to take a large, overwhelming project and break it down into smaller, more manageable steps, a process that is critical for overcoming task paralysis.

- **Simple vs. Complex:** For some, a simple notes app like Apple Notes or Google Keep is enough. You can use it to create quick checklists. For others, a more robust app like **Todoist** or **Trello** is a game-changer. These apps allow you to create subtasks, assign due dates, set priorities, and even link to other files. This turns a vague task like "clean the garage" into a series of actionable steps: "take out trash," "sort tools," "create a donation pile."

- **The Power of Visualization:** Many to-do list apps use visual cues. **Trello**, for example, uses a **Kanban board** system with cards that can be moved from "To Do" to "Doing" to "Done." This visual progression provides a powerful, tangible sense of accomplishment, which releases dopamine and reinforces the positive behavior. It makes your progress visible, which is incredibly motivating.

Calendar Apps: Making Time Tangible

Time blindness makes it difficult to perceive the passage of time, but a digital calendar makes time a tangible, visual entity. Using a digital calendar with color-coding is a highly effective external brain strategy.

- **Color-Coding Your Life:** Assign different colors to different areas of your life (e.g., green for personal appointments, blue for work, yellow for self-care). When you look at your schedule, you can immediately see a visual breakdown of your week. This reduces the mental effort of trying to figure out what's on your plate.

- **The Power of Reminders:** Don't just use your calendar for appointments. Use it to block off your **"focus sprints"** and **"deep dives."** Set up recurring reminders for chores like taking out the trash or watering plants. The reminder acts as a non-judgmental nudge that bypasses your working memory and prompts you to act. The trick is to treat these calendar blocks like a real appointment—a commitment you've made to yourself.

Timers and Habit Trackers: Gamifying Your Routine

The ADHD brain is motivated by novelty, challenge, and reward. Timers and habit trackers are a way to gamify your daily life and turn mundane tasks into engaging, rewarding activities.

- **The Pomodoro Technique:** The Pomodoro Technique is a time-management method that uses a timer to break down work into intervals, traditionally 25 minutes in length, separated by short breaks. There are countless apps dedicated to this method, from simple timers to more elaborate ones that track your progress and provide stats. The timer acts as a constant external anchor for your attention, and the visual countdown helps make time a concrete, perceivable entity.

- **Habit Trackers:** Apps like **Streaks** or **Habitica** can be powerful motivators. The visual representation of your progress, seeing a chain of completed days, provides a powerful dopamine hit and a strong incentive not to break the chain. **Habitica** takes this a step further by turning your life into a role-playing game. You earn "experience points" and "gold" for completing tasks, which you can use to buy in-game items. This harnesses your brain's natural desire for a challenge and a reward in a fun, engaging way.

Automation and Focus: Technology as a Partner

Beyond simple organization, technology can automate tasks and create a more focused environment.

Automation Apps: Reducing Micro-Decisions

Automation is a key strategy for the ADHD brain. It removes the need for a decision, which conserves valuable executive function energy. While there are advanced automation platforms like **Zapier** and **IFTTT** (If This Then That), even your phone's built-in features can be used.

- **Scheduled "Do Not Disturb" Mode:** Set your phone to automatically switch to "Do Not Disturb" mode during your focus sprints or at night. This prevents notifications from hijacking your attention and ensures you have dedicated periods of uninterrupted work or rest.
- **Location-Based Reminders:** Use your phone's built-in reminders to get a notification when you arrive at a specific location. For example, a reminder that says "buy milk" that pops up when you get to the grocery store. This external cue connects the task to the time and place where it can be completed, bypassing your internal memory.

Mindfulness and Focus Apps: Quieting the Noise

For many with ADHD, the internal monologue is a constant source of distraction. The brain is like a crowded, noisy room. Mindfulness and focus apps can act as a way to turn down the volume.

- **Meditation Apps:** Apps like **Headspace** or **Calm** provide guided meditations that can help you practice quieting your mind and returning your focus to the present moment. Even a five-minute session can have a profound impact on your ability to concentrate.

- **White Noise and Ambient Sound Apps:** For some, absolute silence is a distraction. A low, constant sound can help to "fill in the gaps" and prevent the brain from seeking out other, more distracting stimuli. Apps that provide white noise, ambient sounds, or even binaural beats can be an effective way to create a more focused environment.

The Final Word: Curation and Intentionality

The sheer volume of apps available can be a source of overwhelm in itself. The key is to curate your technology. Choose one or two apps for each category, one for your to-do list, one for your calendar, and maybe a timer app. Don't fall into the trap of constantly searching for the "perfect" app. The best app is the one you actually use.

The goal isn't to become a tech wizard; it's to create a small, manageable, and highly effective system. When used strategically, your phone and technology can move from being a source of chaos to being a powerful ally, a trusted partner in your journey toward a more organized and less chaotic life. You are not fighting against your brain's nature; you are building a supportive, external system that allows your unique neurodiversity to shine.

CHAPTER 6:

SEASONAL ROUTINES:
ADAPTING HABITS WITH THE CALENDAR

Why Routines Feel Fragile for ADHD Brains

For many people, routines are sold as the key to order and success: wake up at 5 a.m., drink lemon water, exercise daily, plan your meals, journal, and keep your house spotless. But if you live with ADHD, you probably already know the truth, rigid routines don't last.

You may have set up a perfect morning routine in January, only to see it unravel by February. Or maybe you've tried the same evening checklist a dozen times, each time thinking *this will stick*, only to watch it fall apart after a stressful week or schedule change.

Here's why: ADHD brains are wired for **novelty, flexibility, and adaptation**. They resist monotony and crumble under rigidity. That doesn't mean routines are impossible. It means routines must be **living, breathing structures**, not concrete slabs.

This is where **seasonal routines** come in. By syncing habits to natural cycles, seasons, months, or transitional periods, you create systems that evolve with you instead of breaking when life shifts.

The Seasons as Natural ADHD Anchors

One of the most frustrating parts of ADHD is how time feels slippery. Days blur together. Weeks pass without warning. A month can vanish before you've caught your breath. Seasonal routines solve this by anchoring your habits to the natural markers of the year.

Think of the seasons as built-in **reset buttons**:

- **Spring:** Renewal, decluttering, new projects.
- **Summer:** Activity, lightness, movement.
- **Fall:** Structure, routines, preparation.
- **Winter:** Rest, reflection, coziness.

Instead of fighting the ADHD relationship with time, seasonal routines work with it. They create natural opportunities for refresh and restart, which ADHD brains crave.

Why Seasonal Flexibility Works

Rigid routines fail because they assume life is constant. But ADHDers live in flux, our energy, focus, and motivation rise and fall. Seasonal shifts mirror this ebb and flow, and by adapting routines to them, we create systems that:

1. **Feel new** every few months (satisfying the ADHD need for novelty).
2. **Allow for flexibility** when energy dips or rises.
3. **Break the cycle of shame** by building resets directly into the year.

When you know your routines are *supposed to* change with the season, you stop feeling like a failure when the January plan doesn't work in June. Instead, you adjust. That's not failure, that's design.

Step 1: Identify Seasonal Energy Patterns

The first step is noticing how your energy, focus, and habits shift during the year.

- Do you feel more energized in spring?
- Do summers throw you off with travel and disrupted schedules?
- Does fall feel like a natural time for structure?
- Do winters drain you or invite rest?

Write down your patterns (mentally or on paper). These aren't rules, they're observations. Your unique rhythms will guide how you shape seasonal routines.

Step 2: Anchor Core Habits to Each Season

Every season can hold specific routines that align with its natural energy.

Spring: Renewal & Decluttering

- Open windows for fresh air while cleaning.
- Do a light declutter (a drawer, a closet) to match the "fresh start" energy.
- Rotate clothes and linens (winter away, spring/summer out).
- Use increased daylight to reset wake-up cues.

Spring is ADHD-friendly because it feels new. Lean into that momentum.

Summer: Light & Playful

- Shorter routines to leave room for fun and flexibility.
- Cleaning sprints instead of deep cleans.
- Use outdoor time as natural resets (watering plants, sweeping porches).
- Hydration and sunscreen routines as new anchors.

Summer routines should feel breezy and low-pressure, or they'll collapse.

Fall: Structure & Stability

- Ideal for reintroducing planner use or calendars.
- Weekly resets become anchors as school and work cycles restart.
- Focus on meal prep and cozy home routines.
- Decluttering surfaces and "resetting" spaces before the holiday season.

Fall brings structure naturally: this is the ADHD-friendly time to build frameworks.

Winter: Rest & Reflection

- Simplify routines to bare minimums.
- Use cozy rituals as anchors (tea before bed, lighting candles, soft blankets).
- Short cleaning routines to avoid overwhelm during darker days.
- Annual reset rituals (organizing papers, reviewing budgets, planning the year).

Winter is not about high productivity, it's about sustainable maintenance and recovery.

Step 3: Build Seasonal Reset Rituals

Every season is an invitation to reset. These don't have to be big, they can be simple traditions that signal change.

- **Spring reset:** Swap linens, open windows, donate one bag of clutter.
- **Summer reset:** Pack away school or work clutter, refresh your calendar for lighter weeks.
- **Fall reset:** Buy new notebooks, reset your planner, clear out summer clutter.
- **Winter reset:** Reflect on the year, declutter digital spaces, prepare cozy corners.

These resets act as bookmarks in your year, giving your ADHD brain tangible markers for time and change.

Step 4: Use Seasonal Cues for Motivation

ADHD brains respond to cues. Seasonal shifts bring natural cues you can harness:

- **Smells:** Fall candles, spring flowers, winter spices.
- **Light:** Adjust wake-up routines with changing daylight.
- **Temperature:** Use cozy blankets as evening reset cues, or summer breezes for morning resets.
- **Holidays:** Anchor routines to annual events (Thanksgiving cleaning reset, New Year paper purge).

Instead of resisting these cues, fold them into your systems.

Step 5: Plan for Seasonal ADHD Challenges

Each season brings hurdles. Preparing ahead makes them manageable.

- **Spring:** Overcommitting to too many "fresh start" projects. → Solution: Pick one main focus.
- **Summer:** Disrupted routines due to travel or kids at home. → Solution: Shrink routines to "bare minimums."
- **Fall:** Pressure to be hyper-productive. → Solution: Focus on sustainable systems, not overload.
- **Winter:** Seasonal depression and low motivation. → Solution: Prioritize cozy, minimal routines.

Anticipating challenges makes them less overwhelming when they arrive.

Step 6: Rotate Tools and Systems

Novelty is fuel for ADHD brains. Seasonal routines give permission to swap tools.

- **Spring:** Try a new planner or wall calendar.
- **Summer:** Use sticky notes or digital reminders for short-term goals.
- **Fall:** Reintroduce structured planners or bullet journals.
- **Winter:** Switch to simple to-do lists or cozy routine checklists.

Changing tools seasonally prevents boredom without guilt.

Step 7: Layer Seasonal Habits With Existing Anchors

Anchor seasonal routines to habits you already do.

- In winter, drink tea every night → add "wipe kitchen counter" before pouring.
- In summer, water plants → add "pick up clutter in living room."
- In fall, prep school/work bag nightly → add "10-minute tidy."
- In spring, open windows → add "dust shelves."

Layering keeps routines simple and sustainable.

Step 8: Seasonal Routines for Home Organization

Each season naturally lends itself to different organization projects.

- **Spring:** Closets, wardrobes, storage refresh.
- **Summer:** Outdoor spaces, patios, garages.
- **Fall:** Paperwork, calendars, family command centers.
- **Winter:** Digital files, finances, cozy spaces.

Breaking projects into seasonal chunks prevents overwhelm and creates natural cycles of progress.

Step 9: Family and Household Seasonal Routines

If you live with others, seasonal routines can create shared rhythms.

- **Spring:** Family declutter day (one room together).
- **Summer:** Weekly outdoor cleanup with music.
- **Fall:** Calendar sync and schedule reset.
- **Winter:** Cozy cleanup with hot cocoa afterward.

Shared rituals reduce shame, build teamwork, and make routines feel communal rather than isolating.

Step 10: Seasonal Self-Compassion

Perhaps the most important element of seasonal routines is compassion. ADHD lives are full of ups and downs. Instead of demanding perfection year-round, seasonal routines give you permission to ebb and flow.

- Low energy in winter? That's expected. Simplify.
- Bursting with energy in spring? Ride the wave.
- Distracted in summer? Shrink routines and embrace flexibility.
- Focused in fall? Build structures to carry you through.

When you see yourself as part of a cycle instead of a failure, routines stop being punishments and start being supports.

Case Study 1: Hannah and the Winter Collapse

Hannah always set big January goals: gym five days a week, meal prepping, cleaning routines. By February, she'd burn out and spiral into shame.

When she learned about seasonal routines, she shifted her expectations. Winter became her "maintenance" season. Instead of new goals, she set a cozy evening reset (tidy dishes, light a candle, tea). By spring, she felt refreshed and ready to add bigger habits. Her routines stopped collapsing because they were designed to flex.

Case Study 2: Marcus and the Summer Chaos

Marcus, a teacher with ADHD, loved the structure of the school year but crashed in summer. Without a schedule, his home fell apart.

He adopted summer-specific routines: short 5-minute resets twice a day, paired with outdoor habits (watering plants, sweeping porch). He simplified meal planning to salads and grilled dinners. By embracing seasonal lightness instead of fighting for strict routines, Marcus enjoyed summer without losing control of his space.

Step 11: Seasonal Rituals as ADHD-Friendly Motivation

Rituals are moments of meaning. Seasonal rituals add novelty and joy to routines.

- Spring cleaning day with windows open and favorite playlist.
- Summer reset with iced drinks and 10-minute tidy before heading outside.
- Fall "planner refresh" with new pens and cozy blankets.
- Winter "digital detox day" with cocoa and phone declutter.

These rituals anchor time, add fun, and make routines feel like celebrations.

Closing Thought

ADHD brains are not broken because routines slip. They are wired for movement, novelty, and adaptation. Seasonal routines honor that truth. They turn failure into flexibility, collapse into cycles, and shame into compassion.

Instead of trying to force the same routine year-round, embrace the rhythm of the seasons. Let your routines breathe, bend, and evolve with the calendar. You don't have to fight your brain or the year, you can design systems that work with both.

When you sync your life to the seasons, routines stop being fragile. They become flexible. They stop being punishments. They become support. And that shift changes everything.

CHAPTER 7:

EMERGENCY ROUTINES:
QUICK SYSTEMS FOR CHAOTIC DAYS

Why We Need Emergency Routines

If there's one truth about ADHD life, it's this: some days simply fall apart. The alarm doesn't go off. The kids are melting down. You forgot about the deadline. You're already late, and your house looks like a tornado hit it.

In those moments, standard routines feel impossible. A "perfect morning checklist" is laughable when you're rushing out the door without breakfast. An elaborate evening reset won't happen after a day that leaves you drained and fried.

This is where **emergency routines** save the day. Think of them as the fire extinguishers of daily life: small, fast, bare-minimum systems you pull out when chaos strikes. They aren't glamorous, and they aren't about doing everything "right." They're about keeping life afloat with the least effort possible.

For ADHDers, this matters even more. Without emergency routines, chaotic days spiral into shame spirals: "I failed again. I'll never get this together." With emergency routines, chaotic days become survivable. You have a fallback. You don't need to collapse into guilt.

The Power of "Bare Minimum"

Many ADHDers operate in all-or-nothing mode. Either we clean the entire kitchen top-to-bottom, or we let dishes pile until they're overwhelming. Either we follow our routine perfectly, or we abandon it completely.

Emergency routines break this cycle. They ask: **What's the smallest action that will make life livable today?**

- Instead of "deep clean the kitchen," it's "throw dishes into the sink and rinse."
- Instead of "cook a balanced dinner," it's "order takeout or make a sandwich."
- Instead of "reset the whole house," it's "clear one surface."

By lowering the bar, you still move forward. And forward, even if small, is what breaks the cycle of chaos.

Step 1: The "Three Non-Negotiables"

On the worst days, focus on three things only:

1. **Eat something.** It doesn't have to be healthy or elaborate—just fuel your body.
2. **Hydrate.** ADHD brains forget water, but dehydration makes chaos worse.
3. **Meds (if prescribed).** These are your foundation.

Everything else, laundry, cleaning, emails, comes after. When you strip it down to survival needs, you give yourself grace.

Step 2: Morning Emergency Routine

Mornings can make or break a chaotic day. An emergency morning routine is **fast, minimal, and grounding**.

Example:

- Brush teeth (2 minutes).
- Drink water (30 seconds).
- Dress in something clean and comfortable (5 minutes).
- Grab one food item (banana, granola bar, toast).

That's it. Not a full workout, not journaling, not a perfect breakfast. Just the minimum to leave the house fed, dressed, and semi-functional.

Step 3: Evening Emergency Routine

Evenings are another danger zone. ADHDers often collapse into exhaustion, then wake up to chaos the next morning. An emergency evening routine prevents this spiral.

Example:

- Do a 5-minute "surface sweep" (clear counters or put dishes in sink).
- Plug in devices (phone, laptop).
- Set out clothes for tomorrow.
- Collapse into bed.

Even if the rest of the house is messy, these few actions make tomorrow less overwhelming.

Step 4: Cleaning Emergency Routine

Some days the house feels like it exploded. Instead of thinking *"I have to clean everything,"* use an emergency cleaning system.

The 5-Minute Tidy:

- Set a timer.
- Pick one small area (couch, entryway, kitchen counter).
- Put away only what fits in your hands.
- Stop when timer ends.

The "One Surface Rule":

- Choose one surface (desk, table, counter).
- Clear it completely.
- Celebrate the visible difference.

The Laundry Quick Fix:

- Gather all dirty laundry into one basket.
- Toss one load into washer.
- Don't worry about folding yet.

Cleaning emergencies are about visibility and relief, not perfection.

Step 5: Food Emergency Routine

ADHD brains often forget to eat, or eat chaotically. When life is messy, meals should be **automatic and low-effort**.

- Keep a stash of emergency foods: granola bars, instant noodles, frozen meals, cheese sticks, fruit.
- Use "assembly meals": sandwiches, wraps, quesadillas.
- Order takeout guilt-free when needed.

The goal is not gourmet, it's nourishment. A fed brain is a functioning brain.

Step 6: Work/School Emergency Routine

When deadlines crash and focus is gone, an emergency system keeps you from drowning.

The 15-Minute Start:

- Set a timer.
- Open the assignment or task.
- Work for 15 minutes, no pressure.

Often, starting breaks the paralysis. If it doesn't, you've still done 15 minutes more than nothing.

The "One Thing List":

- Write down the one most urgent task.
- Ignore everything else until it's done.

The Quick Reset:

- Step outside.
- Breathe deeply.
- Return with a clear head.

These routines cut through overwhelm and reduce procrastination spirals.

Step 7: Family and Household Emergency Routines

If you live with others, chaotic days affect everyone. Emergency routines can be communal.

- **Family 10-Minute Cleanup:** Everyone picks one zone. Blast music, clean for 10 minutes, stop.
- **Kid Survival Routines:** Snacks, water, screens for 30 minutes while you reset.
- **Partner Divide-and-Conquer:** One handles food, one handles tidying.

When everyone knows the emergency system, chaos doesn't fall on one person's shoulders.

Step 8: Travel and Out-of-Routine Emergencies

Vacations, holidays, or unexpected events often wreck ADHD systems. Emergency routines keep the basics intact.

- **Travel Bag Anchors:** Pack snacks, meds, chargers, water bottle.
- **Hotel Reset:** Keep clothes in one spot, charge devices in same outlet.
- **Holiday Chaos Plan:** Prioritize food, hydration, and one daily tidy.

Instead of expecting perfect structure, expect disruption, and plan small anchors to survive it.

Step 9: The "Reset in 5" System

Sometimes the whole day has collapsed, and you need a restart. The Reset in 5 is a quick rescue:

1. Drink water.

2. Wash your face or hands.

3. Pick up five items.

4. Open a window or step outside.

5. Write down one next task.

In less than five minutes, you feel fresher, the space looks better, and your brain has direction.

Step 10: Emergency Emotional Routine

Chaotic days aren't just messy, they're emotional. ADHD brains default to guilt and shame when routines collapse. That only makes things harder.

An emotional emergency routine calms the storm:

- Take three deep breaths.
- Say out loud: *"This is temporary. I'm not a failure."*
- Text a supportive friend, or use body doubling.
- Put on a calming or uplifting song.

Soothing yourself is part of survival.

Case Study 1: Maya and the Overloaded Morning

Maya often overslept, then spiraled into panic: she'd skip breakfast, forget her meds, and arrive at work frazzled. Her emergency morning routine became: brush teeth, drink water, grab a granola bar, take meds. Four steps, five minutes. Even on disaster days, she felt grounded.

Case Study 2: Andre and the End-of-Day Crash

Andre came home exhausted from work and collapsed on the couch. Dishes piled up, laundry sat in heaps, and mornings felt unbearable. He adopted an evening emergency routine: put dishes in sink, plug in phone, set out clothes. Ten minutes, then bed. His mornings became calmer, and the house stopped spiraling out of control.

Step 11: Building an Emergency Routine Menu

One of the best ADHD strategies is having a **menu of emergency options**. Instead of relying on memory in crisis, you already know what to do.

Sample Menu:

- Morning: brush teeth, water, clothes, food.
- Evening: 5-minute tidy, plug in devices, clothes out.
- Cleaning: one surface or 5-minute timer.
- Work: one urgent task or 15-minute start.
- Food: granola bar, sandwich, frozen meal.

Print it, post it, or keep it on your phone. When chaos hits, you grab the menu instead of spiraling.

Step 12: Normalize Using Emergency Routines

Emergency routines are not failures. They are **success strategies**. Everyone has days that collapse. The difference is whether you drown in guilt or float with systems.

Think of emergency routines like first aid: you don't use them every day, but when you need them, they save you. And the more you use them, the more you trust yourself to bounce back.

Closing Thought

ADHD life is unpredictable. Routines will fail. Days will collapse. Chaos will come. But chaos doesn't have to mean disaster.

Emergency routines are your life rafts. They are proof that survival doesn't require perfection, just small, simple, compassionate steps. They keep you afloat until calm returns.

And that is the point: you don't have to conquer every day. You only have to rescue it.

Reflection Questions:

- *Book 4 introduced the idea of creating a simple cleaning toolkit and using time-management hacks. Think about your current cleaning routine. What is one item you could add to your cleaning toolkit to make tasks easier, or what is one time-blocking or gamification technique you could try this week to make a specific chore more manageable?*

- *We also discussed delegating, automating, and outsourcing tasks. Is there a recurring chore or mental task that consistently causes you stress (e.g., paying bills, doing laundry)? What is one way you could either automate that task or ask for support to reduce your mental load?*

- *This book presented **"time blindness"** as a common challenge. Is there a specific, recurring task you consistently underestimate the time it will take to complete? What is a small change you could make this week to more accurately schedule that task, either with a timer or a calendar block?*

- *Think about the concept of **dopamine stacking** and making chores fun. What is one of your favorite high-dopamine activities (e.g., listening to a specific podcast, a new snack)? How could you intentionally pair that activity with a low-interest chore this week to make the task more appealing?*

- *We discussed the role of technology as an **"external brain."** What is one recurring thought or reminder that you constantly have to hold in your head (e.g., "I need to buy milk," "I need to call the doctor")? How could you use a simple digital tool, a reminder app, a calendar event, to offload that thought and free up your mental energy?*

BOOK FIVE:

STAYING CONSISTENT AND BOUNCING BACK

CHAPTER 1:

DON'T BREAK THE CHAIN:
VISUAL MOMENTUM TRICKS TO KEEP YOU GOING.

Consistency is the ultimate goal, but for the ADHD brain, it can feel like the most elusive. The "Don't Break the Chain" method is a simple, visual, and highly effective tool for building and maintaining momentum on a new habit. It's a way to gamify consistency and get your brain to focus on a streak, not a single performance. This strategy directly addresses the challenges of **task initiation** and **inconsistency**, which are common symptoms of executive dysfunction. By turning a long-term goal into a short-term, daily challenge, you make consistency a tangible, rewarding experience.

How it Works

The method is simple: get a calendar, a whiteboard, or a simple habit-tracking app. For every day that you successfully perform a new habit—whether it's the "10-minute tidy" or the "evening reset", you place a checkmark or an "X" on that day. The goal is to build a chain of these marks, day after day. The visual representation of the unbroken chain becomes a powerful motivator.

This system works because it makes an abstract concept (**consistency**) concrete and visible. The chain is a physical record of your progress, and it provides a powerful dopamine hit every time you add a new link. It's a non-negotiable, visible cue that serves as a reminder and a reward all in one. The beauty of this method is its simplicity; it doesn't require complex planning or a rigid schedule. It only requires a single, small action each day.

The Psychology Behind It

This method works for the ADHD brain because it taps into several key psychological and neurobiological principles:

- **Visual Cue:** The chain provides a clear, tangible representation of your progress. It's a **dopamine hit** every time you add a new link. The brain is highly motivated by positive reinforcement, and a visual symbol of success provides that immediate reward. For a brain that struggles with working memory, a visual cue is a far more reliable source of motivation than an abstract promise of a "cleaner home someday."

- **Loss Aversion:** This is a powerful cognitive bias where we are more motivated to avoid losing something we have than to gain something we don't. The fear of "breaking the chain" can be a powerful driver to complete the task, even on a day when you don't feel like it. The chain is a visual representation of your effort, and the thought of losing that streak can be a stronger motivator than the initial effort required to start the task.

- **Small, Manageable Task:** The "chain" is not about the monumental task of organizing the entire house. It's about the small, daily action that builds the chain. This keeps the task from feeling overwhelming. By focusing on a single, low-effort habit, you are lowering the activation energy required to start. You are not saying, "I have to clean the whole house"; you are saying, "I just have to do the 10-minute tidy to keep my chain going." This shift in focus is a critical strategy for the ADHD brain.

- **The Power of Habit Stacking:** The "Don't Break the Chain" method is an excellent way to implement **habit stacking**, a strategy where you pair a new habit with an existing, well-established one. For example, if you already have a habit of making your morning coffee, you can "stack" a new habit on top of it. "After I make my coffee, I will do my 10-minute tidy and then check off my chain." This ties the new habit to an existing routine, making it more likely to stick.

The All-or-Nothing Trap and the "Don't Break the Chain" Method

One of the greatest challenges for the ADHD brain is **all-or-nothing thinking**. A single missed day can be interpreted as a complete failure, leading to the abandonment of the habit altogether. The "Don't Break the Chain" method helps to mitigate this. While the goal is an unbroken chain, a single missed day doesn't have to be the end of the world. It's a chance to learn, to adjust, and to start a new chain.

- **Compassionate Re-framing:** If you miss a day, instead of beating yourself up, try to understand why it happened. Was the task too big? Was the time unrealistic? This is a moment for self-compassion and problem-solving, not self-criticism.
- **The "Two-Day Rule":** A helpful rule of thumb is to allow yourself a single missed day, but never two in a row. This prevents a single slip-up from turning into a complete abandonment of the habit. It keeps you focused on the long-term goal without demanding a level of perfection that is unsustainable.

Practical Application: Starting Your First Chain

1. **Choose a Single, Simple Habit:** Don't try to build three new habits at once. Choose one, such as the "10-minute tidy," and commit to it. Make it as easy and low-effort as possible.
2. **Choose Your Tracker:** Find a visual tracker that works for you. A wall calendar is great because it's a constant visual reminder. A simple app is great because it's always with you.
3. **Start with a Small Goal:** Aim for a seven-day chain. The first week is often the hardest, but once you've completed a full week, the momentum is a powerful force.

4. **Celebrate Your Wins:** When you hit a milestone—a full week, a full month—take a moment to celebrate. This provides a crucial dopamine hit and reinforces the positive behavior.

The "Don't Break the Chain" method is not about perfection. It's about showing up, even when it's hard. It's about building a habit one day at a time, and celebrating the visual proof of your consistency. It's a strategy that respects your brain's unique wiring and turns the frustrating pursuit of consistency into a rewarding and achievable game. By using this method, you are building more than just a clean home; you are building a new, more supportive relationship with yourself.

CHAPTER 2:

LIFE HAPPENS — HERE'S THE REBOUND PLAN: HOW TO RECOVER QUICKLY AFTER A SLIP.

No matter how good your systems are, no matter how carefully you plan, life will inevitably get in the way. There will be sick days, travel, busy weeks, and moments when you just fall off the wagon. For the ADHD brain, a slip-up can feel like a total, catastrophic failure, leading to a downward spiral of shame and inaction. The brain's tendency for **all-or-nothing thinking** can turn a single missed day of a routine into a complete abandonment of the habit. This chapter is about learning the art of the rebound, getting back on track without judgment, and understanding that the ability to recover is far more important than the ability to be perfect.

The Myth of "Total Failure"

The myth of "total failure" is a dangerous one. It's the voice in your head that says, "Well, I missed my routine yesterday, so the whole week is a bust. I'll just start again next Monday." This line of thinking is a classic cognitive distortion that prevents progress. It's the idea that if a system isn't perfect, it's worthless.

A missed day is not a total failure. A missed week is not a total failure. It's simply a pause. The most important part of building a routine isn't the ability to never fall off; it's the ability to get back on quickly and without shame. The neurobiological reality is that the prefrontal cortex, which is responsible for self-regulation and long-term planning, is less active in the ADHD brain. When a habit is broken, this part of the brain doesn't have the "go-get-em" energy to say, "That's okay, let's try again." Instead, the emotional centers of the brain can take over, leading to feelings of guilt and shame, which are powerful demotivators. The key to the rebound is to interrupt this cycle before it can take hold.

Think of it like a diet or a workout plan. If you miss one day at the gym, you don't decide that the entire year is a failure. You simply go the next day. The stakes with a chore routine feel different, but the principle is the same. The art of the rebound is a critical skill for building a sustainable, organized life. It's the difference between a temporary slip-up and a permanent derailment.

The "Rebound Rule": Your Non-Negotiable Lifeline

The **"Rebound Rule"** is a simple, non-negotiable principle: **start again tomorrow.** No matter what happened today, no matter what you missed, tomorrow is a new day. You don't have to make up for the missed time or beat yourself up about it. Just wake up and start your routine again, one small step at a time.

This rule is a powerful counter to perfectionism and all-or-nothing thinking. It gives you a clear, simple instruction that doesn't require a complex mental calculus. It's a low-effort way to get back on track.

How to Implement the "Rebound Rule":

1. **Acknowledge, Don't Judge:** The moment you realize you've missed a habit, briefly acknowledge it. Don't get stuck in a shame spiral. A simple mental note like, "I missed my 10-minute tidy today," is enough.

2. **Put it on Tomorrow's List:** Immediately put the habit back on your schedule for the next day. This moves the decision-making from an emotional, in-the-moment choice to a planned, scheduled action. You are making a commitment to your future self.

3. **Make it Tiny:** On the day you rebound, make the first task incredibly small and low-effort. For a "10-minute tidy," maybe you only commit to one minute. The goal isn't to be perfect; the goal is to get started. The act of starting, no matter how small, is a win.

This process works because it bypasses the emotional roadblocks and directly addresses the issue of **task initiation** by making the first step as easy as possible.

Self-Compassion is Key: Quieting the Inner Critic

The journey to an organized life is often derailed not by a lack of ability, but by a lack of **self-compassion**. The inner critic, that voice that tells you you're not good enough or that you're a failure, is a powerful force. This voice is often louder and more persistent for those with ADHD, fueled by a lifetime of perceived shortcomings.

Self-compassion is not an excuse for laziness. It's a deliberate choice to treat yourself with the same kindness and understanding you would offer a friend. Instead of saying, "I should have done better," try, "I did my best today, and tomorrow is another chance to show up for myself." The more compassionate you are with yourself, the easier it is to get back on track. This practice can lower cortisol levels, reduce stress, and create a more conducive mental state for action.

Concrete Examples of Self-Compassion:

- **Instead of:** "I'm so lazy, I didn't even do the dishes."
- **Try:** "I was feeling overwhelmed today, and that's okay. I'll load one dish into the dishwasher now and do the rest in the morning."
- **Instead of:** "I always mess up my routines."
- **Try:** "I'm learning what works for me. My routine didn't fit my energy level today, so I'll try a different approach tomorrow."

This reframing turns a moment of failure into a moment of learning, which is a far more productive and sustainable path.

The "Rebound Toolkit": Specific Strategies for Getting Back on Track

When you find yourself in a slump, a few simple, pre-planned tools can make the rebound process much easier.

- **The Five-Minute Reset:** This is a low-effort, high-impact strategy. Set a timer for five minutes and do a simple task to get a quick win. This could be putting away five items, wiping down a counter, or taking out the trash. The goal is to build momentum, not to complete a major project.

- **The "What I Learned" Journal:** Instead of focusing on what you did wrong, take a moment to reflect on what happened. Was there an external factor, like a lack of sleep? Was the task too big? Write down a short, non-judgmental note about what you learned. This turns a moment of frustration into a moment of data collection, which is invaluable for refining your systems.

- **Body Doubling:** As we discussed in Book 4, the presence of another person, even a virtual one, can provide a powerful anchor for your focus. When you're struggling to get back on track, reach out to a friend or a partner and ask them to "body double" with you. You can both do chores in the same room or on a video call. The social element provides a gentle accountability and a sense of shared purpose that can help you overcome the activation barrier.

- **The "Clean Slate" Method:** When a space becomes so overwhelming that you don't know where to start, try the "clean slate" method. Put everything on a surface into a single box or basket. This gets the visual clutter out of the way immediately. Then, deal with the items in the box one by one. This simple act of containment can provide an immense sense of relief and a clear starting point.

The art of the rebound is a critical skill for building a sustainable, organized life. It's the difference between a temporary slip-up and a permanent derailment. It's about building resilience and a supportive relationship with yourself. By learning to rebound with self-compassion and without judgment, you are building a life that is not only more organized but also more forgiving and more authentically your own.

CHAPTER 3:

YOUR SUPPORT SQUAD:
BUILDING ACCOUNTABILITY THAT ACTUALLY WORKS FOR ADHD.

Trying to build new habits in a vacuum can feel isolating and nearly impossible. The ADHD brain thrives on **external motivation** and support. This is a neurobiological reality. The brain's internal reward and motivation systems, driven by dopamine, are often less consistent. Therefore, an external system, like a friend checking in or a shared goal, can provide the necessary stimulus to initiate and maintain a habit. This chapter is about building a personal "team" of accountability partners and support systems that can help you stay on track, celebrate your wins, and get back up when you fall.

Find an Accountability Partner

An **accountability partner** is someone you check in with regularly to share your goals and your progress. This isn't about judgment; it's about mutual support and gentle pressure. The simple act of telling someone what you're going to do increases your likelihood of doing it. This is a well-documented psychological phenomenon. By externalizing your intentions, you create a social contract that is often a stronger motivator than a personal one.

How to find and work with an accountability partner:

- **Choose Wisely:** Find someone who is supportive, not critical. This could be a friend, a family member, or a fellow ADHD-er. Ideally, you should both be working on a similar goal, as this makes the relationship feel more reciprocal and less one-sided.

- **Establish a Routine:** Schedule a quick 10-minute call or text exchange once a week to share your wins and challenges. Consistency is key here. The routine of the check-in itself becomes a part of the habit.

- **Be Specific:** Instead of saying, "I'm going to be better this week," say, "I am going to do a 10-minute tidy every day after dinner." This gives both of you a clear, measurable goal to discuss.

- **Focus on Progress, Not Perfection:** The purpose of the check-in is not to report a perfect week. It's to be honest about your struggles. An accountability partner is there to help you problem-solve, not to shame you for a slip-up. They can help you brainstorm solutions when your routine isn't working for you.

Body Doubling: The Power of Presence

Body doubling is a specific and highly effective form of accountability. It's the practice of working on a task in the presence of another person, even if they aren't helping. The presence of another person provides a subtle form of accountability and an external anchor for your focus. It helps to regulate your attention and can make a tedious task feel less isolating.

- **In-Person Body Doubling:** This is the most effective form. Ask a friend or partner to work on their own project in the same room while you do your chores. The social element provides a gentle pressure and a sense of shared purpose that can help you overcome the activation barrier.

- **Virtual Body Doubling:** If an in-person partner isn't available, a virtual one can be just as effective. A quick video call with a friend where you both work silently on separate tasks can provide a similar sense of presence and accountability. There are even apps and online communities specifically for this purpose.

The science behind body doubling is fascinating. It's believed that the presence of another person doing a similar task helps to stimulate the **mirror neurons** in our brain. These neurons fire both when we perform an action and when we observe someone else performing the same action, creating a sense of shared purpose and a gentle push toward action.

Leverage Your Support System

Your support system is the community of people who love and care about you: your partner, your family, your close friends. Don't be afraid to lean on them. This is not a sign of weakness; it's a sign of maturity and self-awareness.

- **Communicate Your Needs:** The people who love you want to support you, but they can't read your mind. Explain to your loved ones what you're working on and how they can best support you. This could be as simple as, "I'm trying to be better about my morning routine. Could you remind me to put my keys on the launchpad at night?"

- **Make it a Team Effort:** Frame your organizational journey as a team effort. Instead of saying, "Could you help me clean the kitchen?" say, "Could we work together to get the kitchen clean so we can both relax for the rest of the night?" This shared language of "we" and "our" makes it a collaborative effort rather than a one-sided favor.

- **Ask for Specific, Actionable Help:** Avoid vague requests. Instead of saying, "Help me get organized," ask for specific, actionable help. "Could you spend an hour with me this Saturday to help me go through my closet using the 'Keep, Toss, Donate' method?" This gives your support system a clear, defined way to help you, which makes them more likely to agree.

Professional Support: Therapists and ADHD Coaches

For some, an organized life is a long and winding road that may require professional support. Working with an ADHD coach or a therapist can be a game-changer. These professionals are trained to understand the unique challenges of the ADHD brain and can provide invaluable, personalized strategies.

- **ADHD Coaches:** An ADHD coach specializes in helping individuals develop systems and strategies for managing their symptoms in daily life. They act as a highly specialized accountability partner, helping you set realistic goals, break down tasks, and build sustainable habits. They don't just tell you what to do; they help you find what works for you.
- **Therapists:** A therapist, particularly one who specializes in ADHD, can help you work through the underlying emotional challenges that often accompany ADHD, such as shame, anxiety, and a low sense of self-worth. They can help you reframe your relationship with your brain and develop self-compassion, which is the foundation for all lasting change.

The Power of Community

In addition to one-on-one support, finding a community of people who understand your struggles can be incredibly powerful. Online forums, local support groups, or even social media groups dedicated to ADHD and organization can provide a sense of belonging and a space to share your wins and challenges without judgment. This community can be a source of new ideas, motivation, and the powerful reminder that you are not alone in your journey.

The Final Word: You Are Not a Lone Wolf

Building a support system isn't a sign of weakness; it's a sign of strength. It's a recognition that you don't have to do it all alone and that a team approach is the most effective way to build a sustainable, organized life. By leaning on your accountability partners, your support system, and, if needed, professional help, you are creating a safety net that catches you when you fall and a launchpad that propels you forward when you succeed. The goal isn't to be perfect, but to build a life that is so well-supported that you can thrive, not just survive.

CHAPTER 4:

CELEBRATE EVERY WIN:
HOW SMALL VICTORIES KEEP YOUR BRAIN
MOTIVATED.

For the ADHD brain, the "end of the road" reward, a perfectly organized home, a completely clean garage, can feel so far away that it loses its motivational power. This is because our brains are hardwired to prioritize immediate rewards. This isn't a flaw; it's a feature. The problem with tasks like deep cleaning is that the reward is often abstract and delayed. This is why it's so important to build a system of immediate, smaller rewards. This chapter is about acknowledging and celebrating your wins, no matter how small they are, to keep your brain engaged and motivated.

Think of it like a video game. You don't have to beat the final boss to get a reward. Every small enemy you defeat, every coin you collect, every level you complete gives you a small, immediate win that encourages you to keep going. We are going to apply that same principle to the tasks in your home.

The Neurobiology of Celebration: The Dopamine Feedback Loop

The ADHD brain is driven by **dopamine**, a neurotransmitter that plays a crucial role in motivation, reward, and pleasure. When we complete a task and immediately celebrate that win, we are giving our brain a dose of that feel-good chemical. This creates a powerful **positive feedback loop**:

1. You start a task.
2. You complete a small part of it.
3. You immediately celebrate the win.
4. Your brain releases dopamine, which makes you feel good.
5. This positive feeling is then associated with the task, making it more likely that you will want to do it again.

This is a deliberate, neurobiologically-informed strategy. By celebrating a win, you're not just being self-indulgent; you're actively reinforcing the neural pathways for the new habit, making it easier and more automatic over time. You are training your brain to see these tasks not as tedious chores, but as opportunities for a reward.

The Power of Immediate Gratification

The key to this system is making the reward immediate and aligned with the effort. The reward should be a low-effort, high-impact experience that provides an immediate dopamine hit.

Verbal Acknowledgment: The Power of Self-Praise

Verbal acknowledgment is the simplest, most immediate form of celebration. When you finish a task, say out loud, "I did it!" This simple act of self-praise reinforces the positive behavior. It's an external cue that acknowledges your effort and makes your achievement concrete.

- **Make it a Habit:** The moment you finish putting away the last dish, say, "Done!" or "Boom! Another win." This simple verbal tag reinforces the feeling of accomplishment.
- **The Power of Framing:** Instead of just acknowledging the task, acknowledge your effort. Say, "I did a great job sticking to my 10-minute tidy today," or "I really showed up for myself

by getting that done." This builds a positive self-narrative that is more motivating than a negative one.

This may feel silly at first, but it is a powerful way to train your brain. It is the verbal equivalent of a checkmark on a to-do list.

Small, Tangible Rewards: A Guilt-Free Treat

After a small win, a small, tangible reward can be a powerful motivator. The key here is to make the reward immediate, easy to access, and not so big that it becomes a distraction.

- **After a 15-minute cleaning sprint:**
  - Enjoy a piece of your favorite dark chocolate.
  - Watch one episode of a show you're currently watching.
  - Spend a few minutes playing a video game you enjoy.
  - Sit down for a few minutes with a special cup of tea or coffee.
- **After a "deep dive" project:**
  - Treat yourself to a movie night.
  - Order your favorite takeout for dinner.
  - Take a long, hot bath with a podcast playing.
  - Go for a walk in a place you love.

The reward should be **guilt-free**. It is not a sign of laziness; it is a strategic investment in your future motivation. You're giving your brain the encouragement it needs to keep going. It's a way of saying, "Thank you for the hard work, here's a little something for you."

Visual Proof: The Motivation You Can See

For the ADHD brain, which is often highly visual, seeing your progress is a powerful motivator. The chain on a habit tracker, a clean counter, or a tidied room provides a dopamine hit that can be revisited when you're feeling unmotivated.

- **Before-and-After Photos:** Take a picture of a messy space before you start a project and another one after you're done. The visual contrast is a powerful, tangible record of your accomplishment. Look at these pictures when you're feeling a lack of motivation.

- **The Habit Tracker:** As we discussed in Book 5, the visual chain of "X's" on a calendar is a powerful reward in itself. The longer the chain gets, the more motivated you are to keep it from breaking. This visual proof of your consistency is a testament to your hard work.
- **A "Trophy" Shelf:** For a project you're particularly proud of, put a small item, a toy, a piece of art, on a designated "trophy shelf." This is a physical, visual reminder of your ability to complete a task.

These visual cues bypass the need for memory and self-motivation by providing an immediate, powerful reminder of your success.

Advanced Celebration Strategies

Once you've mastered the basics, you can build on them with more advanced strategies.

The "Win of the Day" Ritual

At the end of each day, take just one minute to reflect on a single "win." It doesn't have to be a major accomplishment. It could be something as simple as, "I remembered to put the keys on the launchpad," or "I successfully completed my 10-minute tidy." This ritual of reflection is a powerful way to reframe your day from a series of perceived failures to a series of small wins. It trains your brain to look for the positive, which can have a profound impact on your overall mindset.

Connect Wins to Values: The "Why" of the Win

For a deeper sense of motivation, try connecting a small win to a larger value. This adds a layer of meaning that can be incredibly powerful.

- **Instead of:** "I did the dishes."
- **Try:** "I did the dishes, which is an act of self-care and helps create a more peaceful, beautiful home for myself."
- **Instead of:** "I paid that bill on time."
- **Try:** "I paid that bill on time, which is a great way to show responsibility and reduce future anxiety."

This reframing moves the task from a simple chore to an action that is aligned with your deeper values, which can be a more sustainable source of motivation.

The Celebration Calendar

Create a simple calendar that is separate from your chore list. On this calendar, mark down every win, big or small. This calendar becomes a visual record of your successes, not just your obligations. It's a powerful reminder that your life is a series of wins, not just a series of challenges.

The All-or-Nothing Trap and the "Rebound"

The all-or-nothing trap is the voice that says, "I didn't get all the dishes done, so it doesn't count." This is the enemy of progress. Celebration is the perfect counter. Celebrate the fact that you did *some* of the dishes. Celebrate the fact that you started. The act of celebrating is a signal to your brain that effort is the important part, not perfection.

This ties back to the **"Rebound Rule"** from Chapter 2. When you do fall off the wagon, you can use celebration as a tool to get back on. Celebrate the fact that you're choosing to rebound. The act of returning to a habit after a slip-up is a huge win, and it deserves to be celebrated.

The Final Word: You Are Worthy of Celebration

Celebrating your wins isn't about being self-indulgent; it's about being strategic. You're giving your brain the encouragement it needs to keep going. You are not fighting against your brain's nature; you are working with it, using its need for immediate gratification to build long-term, sustainable habits. By building a system of immediate, tangible rewards, you are training your brain to see your tasks not as obstacles, but as opportunities for a win. You are building a new, more supportive relationship with yourself, and that is a reward in itself.

CHAPTER 5:

YOUR ORGANIZED FUTURE:
CREATING A HOME AND LIFE THAT STAYS
MANAGEABLE FOR THE LONG HAUL.

As we reach the end of this journey, it's important to remember that organization is not a destination. It's a continuous practice of building systems, being flexible, and showing yourself compassion. This book has given you a toolkit, but you are the architect. Your organized future is not a perfectly clean home; it's a home that feels peaceful, functional, and supportive of your unique brain.

Redefining Your Relationship with Organization

For many people, the word "organization" conjures images of pristine, minimalist spaces, color-coded shelves, and an impossibly tidy aesthetic. For the ADHD brain, this vision can be a source of shame and overwhelm. It sets an unrealistic standard that is often based on the neurotypical brain's capacity for routine and sustained attention. The first step toward your organized future is to let go of this myth.

Your organized future isn't about perfection; it's about **functionality**. It's about a system that works for you, not against you. Your home is not a museum to be admired; it's a launchpad for your life. The goal is to reduce the friction in your daily existence so that your limited mental energy can be directed toward what truly matters: your relationships, your career, your passions, and your well-being. This is an identity shift. You are moving from a person who *struggles* with organization to a person who *maintains* systems that support your life.

The Functional Home: A Sanctuary for Your Brain

What does a functional home actually look like for someone with ADHD? It's a home that is designed with your specific neurobiology in mind. It's a home that understands your need for visual calm, your challenges with working memory, and your brain's craving for novelty and reward.

The "Visual Calm" of a Low-Friction System

One of the most powerful concepts in this book is the idea of a **low-friction system**. A low-friction system is one that requires minimal mental energy to use. Think of the "launchpad" for your keys and wallet. The friction of hunting for them is gone. Your organized future is a home filled with these low-friction systems.

- **Open-Face Storage:** For many with ADHD, "out of sight, out of mind" is a constant reality. Closed cabinets and opaque boxes can be a death sentence for organization. Your functional home will likely use more open-face storage, like clear bins or open shelves, so that you can see what you have. This externalizes the need to remember where things are.

- **The "One-Touch Rule":** This is a simple principle to live by. When you bring an item into your home, it should only be touched once before it is put in its proper place. This is a difficult habit to build, but it's the cornerstone of a functional home. It prevents the pile-up of mail, clothes, and other items that create a "chaos hotspot."

- **Zones of Function:** Your organized future doesn't have perfectly clean rooms; it has functional **zones**. Your entryway is the "launchpad" zone. Your kitchen counter is the "prep zone." Your desk is the "focus zone." By defining these zones, you are giving each space a clear purpose, which reduces the mental effort required to know what to do in that space.

Your functional home is a sanctuary, not because it is perfectly tidy, but because it is designed to support you. It's a space where you are in control, not overwhelmed by the demands of a chaotic environment.

The Journey from Shame to Self-Compassion

Perhaps the most significant journey you will take is the one from shame to self-compassion. Many people with ADHD have spent a lifetime internalizing a narrative of "failure." You've been told you're lazy, unmotivated, or just not trying hard enough. This book has hopefully shown you that these are not character flaws, but symptoms of a unique neurotype.

Your organized future is a life where you have replaced shame with **self-compassion**. A slip-up is just a slip-up, not a total failure. The "Rebound Rule" is not just a scheduling hack; it's a profound act of self-forgiveness. It's the moment you say to yourself, "I am a human being, I did my best today, and tomorrow is another chance to show up for myself."

- **Acknowledge the Pain:** The first step to self-compassion is acknowledging the pain of past struggles. It's okay to recognize that it has been a hard journey. Acknowledging this pain is not a sign of weakness; it's a sign of strength and a necessary step toward healing.

- **Reframe the Narrative:** Instead of seeing past struggles as a sign of personal failure, reframe them as moments of learning.

The messy closet wasn't a sign that you are a bad person; it was a sign that the system you were using wasn't working for you. Your organized future is built on these lessons, not on a foundation of guilt.

- **Forgive Yourself:** Practice forgiving yourself for the times you fell off the wagon. You were doing the best you could with the tools you had. Now you have a new toolkit, and with it comes a new chance to build a better future.

This journey of self-compassion is the emotional engine that will power your long-term success. It's the difference between a system that is a source of anxiety and one that is a source of peace.

Your Personal Playbook: The Art of the Architect

This book is a collection of blueprints, not a finished house. You are the architect. The "Don't Break the Chain" method, the "Beat the Clock" game, the cleaning caddy—these are all tools. Your job is to experiment, iterate, and build a personalized system that works for your unique brain.

- **Start Small and Iterate:** Don't try to implement every strategy at once. Pick one small, low-effort habit, like the "One-Song Tidy," and try it for a week. If it works, great. If not, try another one. This is a process of scientific discovery, not a race to perfection.

- **Listen to Your Brain:** Pay attention to what works and what doesn't. When a system fails, don't blame yourself. Ask, "What did I learn from this?" The answer might be, "I learned that I hate doing dishes, so maybe I should look into outsourcing that." Or, "I learned that visual timers are more effective for me than my phone timer."

- **The "Maintenance Mindset":** The most powerful identity shift you can make is to stop thinking of organization as a one-time event and start thinking of it as a continuous practice. You are not "getting organized"; you are "maintaining my systems." The 10-minute tidy isn't a chore; it's the daily maintenance of your system. This small shift in language can have a profound impact on your motivation and consistency.

This is a powerful and empowering vision. You are not a passive victim of your neurodiversity; you are an active agent, a designer, a problem-solver. You are building a life that is tailored to your unique strengths and needs.

The Universal Message: A Call to Action

While this book has been a guide for men with adult ADHD, its lessons are universal. They are for anyone who has ever felt overwhelmed by a chaotic world, for anyone who has ever felt shame for not living up to an impossible standard.

This book is a call to action: to stop fighting your brain and start working with it. Embrace your neurodiversity, celebrate your unique gifts, and continue to build the extraordinary life you are capable of living. Your organized future is not a destination to be reached; it is a journey to be enjoyed, one small, compassionate step at a time. It is a life where your home is a source of peace, not stress, and where you have the mental space to focus on the things that make you feel alive.

CHAPTER 6:

MOMENTUM BUILDERS:
RESTARTING AFTER FALLING OFF TRACK

Why ADHD Makes Consistency Hard

If you live with ADHD, you already know the story: you start something with excitement, energy, and hope. A new planner, a new exercise routine, a new cleaning system: it feels like *this time, it's going to stick.* For a while, it works. Then life happens. You get sick, your schedule changes, your interest wanes, or something stressful throws you off course. Suddenly, the habit is gone.

Here's the painful part: ADHD brains often don't just stop the habit, they pile guilt and shame on top. "I ruined it. I'll never be consistent. I'm broken." The shame becomes heavier than the original task.

But here's the truth: **falling off track isn't failure—it's inevitable.** Everyone, ADHD or not, falls off routines. The difference is that neurotypical brains tend to slip back more easily, while ADHD brains get caught in the restart trap. We interpret a break as the end. Restarting feels like climbing Mount Everest in flip-flops.

That's why this chapter matters. Momentum isn't about never stopping. It's about learning to **restart quickly, gently, and without shame.**

The Myth of "Forever Consistency"

One reason ADHDers get stuck is the myth that "real consistency" means *never missing a day.* That's not realistic for anyone. Athletes miss workouts. Writers miss writing days. Parents miss routines. Life happens.

What matters is not perfection, but **returning**. Consistency is the art of coming back. And for ADHDers, this means designing momentum builders, small, powerful tools to restart without shame spirals.

Why Restarting Feels Impossible for ADHD

Before we dive into solutions, let's break down why restarting is so hard:

1. **Time blindness.** A "two-day break" might feel like two months. It's easy to believe too much time has passed to restart.

2. **Perfectionism.** If you can't restart "perfectly," it doesn't feel worth trying at all.

3. **Shame spiral.** Falling off track feels like failure, which makes action harder.

4. **Boredom/novelty seeking.** Restarting feels dull compared to starting something new.

5. **Task initiation difficulty.** Restarting is essentially starting again—and starting is the hardest part with ADHD.

Recognizing these barriers isn't about blame, it's about clarity. When you know the obstacles, you can design momentum builders to overcome them.

Momentum Builder #1: The Tiny Restart

When restarting feels overwhelming, shrink the restart step until it feels laughably small.

- Haven't cleaned in weeks? Pick up **one item.**
- Haven't worked out? Do **one stretch.**
- Haven't journaled? Write **one sentence.**
- Haven't studied? Open the book for **one minute.**

Tiny restarts break through the wall of initiation. The brain shifts from *"I can't do this"* to *"Well, that wasn't so bad."* Often, the small action snowballs. But even if it doesn't, you've restarted, and that's momentum.

Momentum Builder #2: The Fresh Start Ritual

ADHD thrives on novelty. Instead of trying to drag yourself back into the old habit, create a ritual that marks a new beginning.

- Light a candle before restarting your evening routine.
- Put on a favorite playlist before tackling the kitchen.
- Buy a new pen before reopening your planner.
- Declare out loud: *"I'm starting again."*

Rituals shift the restart from punishment to celebration. They remind your brain that starting again is renewal.

Momentum Builder #3: Lower the Bar Permanently

One reason we fall off track is that the habit was too ambitious to begin with. The restart then feels impossible. Lowering the bar ensures the habit is resilient.

- Instead of daily workouts, aim for two per week.
- Instead of cleaning the whole kitchen nightly, aim for clearing one counter.
- Instead of journaling a page, aim for one line.

When the bar is lower, the restart doesn't feel like climbing Everest. It feels like stepping back onto a sidewalk.

Momentum Builder #4: The "Restart Menu"

In chaos, ADHD brains forget options. A restart menu is a pre-made list of tiny, easy actions you can choose from.

Example Restart Menu:

- Drink a glass of water.
- Put laundry in basket.
- Write one to-do.
- Wipe one surface.
- Take meds.

Keep your menu on the fridge, in your phone, or taped to your desk. On restart days, don't overthink, just pick one and begin.

Momentum Builder #5: Gamify the Restart

ADHD brains crave dopamine. Restarting feels boring, so inject novelty and fun.

- Set a timer: "Can I clean for 3 minutes?"
- Race yourself: "Can I beat yesterday's restart?"
- Use apps that track streaks, but count restarts as wins.
- Reward yourself for restarting, not for perfect streaks.

The goal is to make restarting stimulating instead of shameful.

Momentum Builder #6: The "Future Me" Perspective

ADHD brains live in the now. Restarting feels pointless because the payoff is delayed. Reframe it as a gift to your **future self.**

- *"Future me will thank me for putting this load of laundry in."*
- *"Future me will feel better if I restart this planner."*
- *"Future me will be calmer if I wipe this counter."*

Speaking directly to the future makes the action more immediate and motivating.

Momentum Builder #7: Body Doubling

Restarting alone feels daunting. With another person, even virtually, it becomes manageable.

- Ask a friend to body double on video while you restart.
- Join a study-with-me stream.
- Sit near a family member while doing your task.

Accountability transforms restart energy. Suddenly, you're not alone, you're supported.

Momentum Builder #8: Reset the Environment

Physical environment cues mental restart.

- Open windows for fresh air.
- Clear one surface.
- Change your workspace location.
- Put on a new outfit.

Environmental resets signal to your brain: *something has shifted, it's time to begin again.*

Momentum Builder #9: "Forgiveness First"

The heaviest barrier to restarting is shame. Before taking action, pause and forgive yourself.

Say out loud:

- *"I'm not broken. Everyone falls off."*
- *"Restarting is progress."*
- *"I don't have to earn permission to try again."*

Forgiveness clears the emotional clutter so action feels possible.

Momentum Builder #10: Seasonal Restarts

Instead of expecting habits to run nonstop, build restarts into seasonal cycles.

- Spring: refresh routines with new energy.
- Summer: simplify to light, minimal routines.
- Fall: rebuild structure with calendars and planners.
- Winter: reduce to bare minimums, focus on rest.

When restart is scheduled, it's no longer a failure, it's design.

Case Study 1: Lila and the Exercise Spiral

Lila joined a gym in January, went three times a week, then stopped when work got stressful. Months passed. She felt guilty, avoided the gym, and told herself she was a failure.

Then she used the **tiny restart**: one five-minute walk. That one walk became two. Then a class. Soon she was moving again. The key was lowering the restart barrier.

Case Study 2: Daniel and the Planner Shame

Daniel bought a beautiful planner, used it for three weeks, then stopped. Months later, he looked at it and thought, *I wasted my money. I can't stick to anything.*

Instead of throwing it away, he used the **fresh start ritual**: he bought a new pen, decorated one page, and wrote just one task. Suddenly the planner wasn't a symbol of failure, it was alive again.

Momentum Builder #11: Celebrate the Restart, Not the Streak

Traditional advice praises streaks. But streaks set ADHDers up for heartbreak, miss one day, and the streak is "ruined." Instead, celebrate restarts.

- Missed five days? Restarted today. That's a win.
- Restarted laundry after a month? Win.
- Restarted journaling after six months? Win.

Consistency is not how many days you never miss, it's how many times you restart.

Momentum Builder #12: Visual Progress Anchors

ADHD brains thrive on visual cues. Use them to make restarts satisfying.

- A calendar with restart days marked in bright colors.
- A jar where you drop a marble every time you restart.
- Before-and-after photos of small resets.

Visual proof creates momentum when your brain forgets progress.

Momentum Builder #13: Pair Restarts With Dopamine

Link restarts with pleasure to make them stick.

- Restarting cleaning? Play your favorite upbeat song.
- Restarting a workout? Pair with your best podcast.
- Restarting a planner? Use colorful pens and stickers.

When restarts feel enjoyable, your brain seeks them instead of avoiding them.

Momentum Builder #14: Emergency Restart Routine

Sometimes life implodes, and you need a one-size-fits-all rescue plan.

The 5-Step Emergency Restart:

1. Drink water.
2. Pick up 5 things.
3. Do one tiny self-care task (wash face, meds, snack).
4. Write one next step.
5. Celebrate restarting.

This sequence can be used anytime you feel stuck in paralysis.

Momentum Builder #15: Build "Restart Resilience"

The more you practice restarting, the easier it becomes. Instead of fearing the next fall, expect it, and trust your restart system.

- Miss a day? Restart tomorrow.
- Miss a week? Restart next week.
- Miss a month? Restart next month.

Restarting isn't failure. It's resilience.

Deep Dive: The Psychology of Restarting

Let's zoom in on why these momentum builders work.

- **Dopamine regulation:** ADHD brains struggle with dopamine. Novelty, gamification, and rewards make restarting engaging.

- **Task initiation:** Shrinking tasks lowers the activation barrier.
- **Time blindness:** Visual cues and seasonal resets anchor the sense of time.
- **Emotional regulation:** Forgiveness and rituals reduce shame, making action easier.
- **Executive function:** Menus, body doubling, and environmental resets scaffold weak executive skills.

Restarting becomes less about willpower and more about designing systems that bypass ADHD roadblocks.

Case Study 3: Sofia and the Cleaning Collapse

Sofia's home would swing between spotless and disaster. After a busy week, the mess piled up. Instead of restarting, she'd spiral into shame, avoid cleaning, and the house worsened.

She built a **restart menu**: pick up 5 things, wipe one surface, start laundry. Every time she fell off, she chose one menu item. Slowly, her home stopped collapsing into chaos. Restarts became her momentum.

Case Study 4: Malik and the Writing Project

Malik wanted to write a book. He wrote daily for a month, then stopped. For six months, he avoided it, convinced he'd failed.

Then he tried the **tiny restart**: write one sentence. That sentence became a paragraph. Weeks later, he was writing regularly again. The book didn't die, it paused, then restarted.

Closing Thought

Consistency isn't the absence of failure. It isn't never missing a day. For ADHDers, consistency is the **courage to restart, again and again.**

Momentum isn't about flawless streaks. It's about building resilience into your systems so falling off doesn't mean the end. It means a pause. A cycle. A chance to begin again.

Every time you restart, you prove something powerful: You are not broken. You are adaptable. You are resilient.

And in the end, resilience, not perfection, is what keeps momentum alive.

CHAPTER 7:

CONSISTENCY THROUGH VARIETY:
CHANGING SYSTEMS WITHOUT QUITTING

The ADHD Struggle With Consistency

If there's one thing that makes ADHD brains grind against traditional advice, it's the idea that consistency means doing the **same thing, the same way, every day, forever.**

You've probably heard it before: *Pick a planner and stick to it. Find a cleaning system and never change it. Pick a workout routine and do it religiously.*

But here's the truth: ADHD brains are wired for **novelty, stimulation, and change.** What feels like security to a neurotypical brain often feels like suffocation to an ADHD brain. Doing the same routine every day, with no variation, quickly becomes dull. Once the dopamine wears off, the system collapses.

That doesn't mean consistency is impossible. It means we need a new definition:

For ADHD, consistency doesn't mean sameness. It means continuity - showing up again and again, even if the *form* of the system changes.

This is the heart of **consistency through variety.** Instead of trying to force one rigid system forever, you design flexible systems that evolve with your brain's needs.

Redefining Consistency

Before we dive into strategies, let's shift the definition. Traditional consistency = "Do the same task the same way daily, no excuses."

ADHD consistency = "Keep coming back to the goal, even if the method shifts."

- If you journal using a notebook one month, a phone app the next, and voice memos after that, you're still journaling consistently.
- If you exercise with yoga for two weeks, then walk for three weeks, then dance for a month, you're still consistently moving your body.
- If you clean your house using a checklist one season, a visual reset system the next, and a timer method after that, you're still consistently maintaining your home.

Consistency is not about the **tool.** It's about the **direction.**

Why Variety Works for ADHD Brains

Variety isn't a weakness, it's a superpower when channeled intentionally. Here's why it works:

1. **Novelty fuels dopamine.** New systems feel exciting, which motivates action.

2. **Flexibility prevents collapse.** When one system feels stale, variety gives you alternatives instead of total abandonment.

3. **Prevents all-or-nothing spirals.** Instead of quitting, you pivot.

4. **Builds resilience.** By using different methods, you discover multiple ways to reach the same goal.

5. **Honors energy cycles.** Different seasons of life (and seasons of the year) require different systems.

By embracing variety, you stop fighting your ADHD wiring and start working with it.

The Danger of Variety Without Intention

Of course, there's a flip side. ADHDers often chase novelty endlessly, abandoning systems as soon as the shine wears off. This leads to clutter (five unused planners, three apps), wasted money, and a sense of failure.

The difference between **chaotic variety** and **intentional variety** is one key rule:

- Chaotic variety = quitting and starting over every time.
- Intentional variety = rotating tools and methods while staying anchored to the same underlying goal.

This chapter is about building intentional variety, consistency through change.

Strategy 1: Anchor to the Core Habit, Not the Tool

Instead of tying consistency to one tool, anchor it to the outcome.

- The core habit is **movement.** Tools may be yoga, walking, dancing.
- The core habit is **planning.** Tools may be a notebook, an app, a whiteboard.
- The core habit is **cleaning.** Tools may be checklists, sprints, or visual resets.

By defining the habit broadly, you give yourself freedom to rotate tools without guilt.

Strategy 2: Create a Rotation System

Think of your systems like a wardrobe. You don't wear one outfit forever, you rotate based on weather, season, and mood. Systems can work the same way.

- **Planners:** Paper journal in winter, digital app in summer.
- **Exercise:** Indoor routines in cold months, outdoor walks in warm months.
- **Cleaning:** Deep cleaning bursts in spring, quick maintenance resets in busy fall.

Rotation prevents burnout and keeps habits alive.

Strategy 3: Build "Novelty Days" Into Routines

Instead of abandoning a system when it feels stale, schedule novelty into it.

- Use themed cleaning days (Music Monday, Timer Tuesday, Flash-Clean Friday).
- Try new recipes once a week while keeping regular meals the rest of the time.
- Rotate pens, colors, or stickers in your planner for visual novelty.
- Once a month, completely change the setting for your work (coffee shop, park, library).

Novelty days refresh the brain without dismantling the system.

Strategy 4: Use Parallel Systems

Some ADHDers thrive with multiple options running at once.

Example: Planning systems.

- Daily tasks go in a paper notebook.
- Weekly overview on a whiteboard.
- Long-term appointments in Google Calendar.

This layered approach provides variety while ensuring you always have a system running. If one tool fails, another catches you.

Strategy 5: Seasonal System Swaps

ADHD thrives on cycles. Just as seasons change, your systems can too.

- **Spring:** Energizing routines, fresh starts.
- **Summer:** Light, flexible systems.
- **Fall:** Structured planners, stability.
- **Winter:** Simplified, cozy routines.

Design seasonal swaps so change is expected, not shameful.

Strategy 6: The "Toolkit Approach"

Think of your routines as a **toolkit, not a prison.**

Your cleaning toolkit might include:

- 5-minute sprints
- One-surface resets
- Checklists
- Body doubling

You don't have to use all at once. On any given day, pick the tool that fits your energy. Consistency comes from showing up, not from using the same hammer every time.

Strategy 7: Differentiate "Healthy Variety" From Avoidance

Sometimes switching systems is a healthy adaptation. Other times it's avoidance. How to tell the difference?

- **Healthy variety** keeps you moving toward the goal. (Switching from yoga to walking, still moving your body.)
- **Avoidance variety** abandons the goal completely. (Stopping workouts and calling it a "system change.")

Ask yourself: *Am I still moving toward the same outcome, or am I abandoning it entirely?*

Strategy 8: Reframe Abandoned Systems as "Chapters"

When a system no longer works, instead of calling it failure, call it a chapter.

- *"That planner worked for me in Fall 2023. That chapter is closed. Now it's Winter 2024, and I'm writing a new chapter."*

This language shifts the narrative from shame to evolution. Systems aren't wasted—they served their season.

Strategy 9: Gamify Variety

Turn system shifts into a game instead of guilt.

- Rate your current system on a scale of 1–10.
- When it dips below 5, swap to a new one.
- Keep a "variety log" of all the systems you've tried. Celebrate the creativity.

The goal is not to lock yourself into one method, but to see how many creative ways you can move toward the same outcome.

Case Study 1: Emma and the Planner Pile

Emma had six half-used planners on her shelf. Each time she abandoned one, she felt guilty and told herself she was a failure.

When she reframed consistency as continuity, she realized each planner was part of her journey. She started rotating between a bullet journal and Google Calendar, depending on her energy. Instead of guilt, she saw variety as strategy.

Case Study 2: Jordan and Exercise Burnout

Jordan joined a gym and followed a strict weightlifting program. After three weeks, he quit, bored out of his mind.

With the **consistency through variety** approach, he designed a rotation: dancing on Mondays, yoga on Wednesdays, hiking on weekends. He never stuck to one workout for long, but he consistently moved his body year-round.

Strategy 10: Visualize Consistency as a Spiral, Not a Line

Neurotypical consistency is imagined as a straight line: same step, every day. ADHD consistency works better as a spiral. You circle around the same goal again and again, sometimes closer, sometimes further, but always returning.

This spiral view reframes restarts as part of the design, not failure.

Strategy 11: Celebrate "Consistency of Return"

Instead of measuring how long you did something without stopping, measure how many times you came back.

- Journaling for 3 months, stopping, then returning a year later? That's consistency of return.
- Cleaning your house in bursts every season? That's consistency of return.
- Using five different planners in five years? That's consistency of return.

What matters is not the gap, it's the return.

Strategy 12: Build Variety Into Rewards

Rewards fuel ADHD motivation. Instead of one static reward, rotate them.

- After cleaning: sometimes a favorite show, sometimes a snack, sometimes a call with a friend.
- After workouts: new music one week, a smoothie the next.
- After journaling: stickers, colored pens, or sharing with a friend.

Changing rewards keeps systems fresh.

Strategy 13: Social Variety

ADHDers thrive on interaction. Bring variety through people.

- Clean alone some days, with a friend others.
- Join a coworking group once a week.
- Share progress with different accountability buddies.

Different people bring different energy, keeping routines lively.

Strategy 14: Use "System Audits"

Every month or season, do a quick audit:

- What's working?
- What feels stale?
- What needs a swap?

Instead of waiting for burnout, you proactively refresh systems.

Case Study 3: Leah and Cleaning Resets

Leah tried a strict "clean the kitchen every night" rule. It lasted two weeks, then collapsed. Instead of giving up, she created a variety system:

- Mondays = 10-minute kitchen sprint.
- Wednesdays = clean one surface.
- Fridays = family reset.

The variation kept her engaged, and the kitchen stayed consistently manageable.

Strategy 15: The "Playlist Effect"

Think of routines like playlists. You don't listen to one song on repeat forever. You rotate songs, shuffle, add new ones. But the playlist is still yours.

Your routines can be playlists too: rotating methods, refreshing with new tools, but always anchored to the same beat.

Deep Dive: The Neuroscience of Variety

ADHD brains have lower baseline dopamine and higher novelty-seeking behavior. That's why:

- New planners feel thrilling.
- New workouts feel exciting.
- New apps feel irresistible.

But once novelty fades, motivation crashes. Intentional variety prevents the crash by supplying novelty in controlled doses. Instead of abandoning systems, you rotate them to sustain dopamine long-term.

Case Study 4: Carlos and Study Routines

Carlos was a college student with ADHD. He tried flashcards, quit. Tried apps, quit. Tried study groups, quit.

Once he reframed consistency, he realized he wasn't failing, he was building a **study toolkit.** Some weeks he used flashcards, others study groups, others apps. He passed his exams not because he stuck to one system, but because he rotated systems and kept returning to the goal.

Closing Thought

ADHD consistency will never look like rigid repetition. And it doesn't need to.

Consistency for us means returning again and again, even if the path shifts. It means designing routines that breathe, flex, and evolve with our brains. It means variety not as avoidance, but as strategy.

When you embrace consistency through variety, you stop seeing yourself as broken for "not sticking with it." You see yourself as creative, resilient, and adaptive.

You are not failing when you change systems—you are succeeding when you keep showing up.

And that's the truth: **Consistency isn't sameness. Consistency is return.**

Reflection Questions:

- *The "Don't Break the Chain" method and the "Art of the Rebound" are two sides of the same coin when it comes to consistency. What is one small habit you want to start building, and how will you use both a visual "chain" and a self-compassionate "rebound rule" to ensure a slip-up doesn't derail your progress?*

- *This final book is about building a supportive, sustainable life. Who is one person in your life you can enlist as an accountability partner or support system for your new organizational goals? What is a small win you've had recently that you will take a moment to celebrate?*

- *This book presented a vision of your organized future as one of functionality, not perfection. In what specific area of your life could you let go of a perfectionistic ideal and instead focus on creating a system that is simply good enough and functional for your brain?*

- *Think about the concept of a "functional home." What is one small change you could make to a "chaos hotspot" in your home (e.g., your entryway, kitchen counter, or desk) to make it a more supportive and low-friction space for your daily life?*
- *What is one core takeaway from this book that you will commit to remembering when a moment of frustration or self-doubt arises? How can this new understanding help you reframe that moment with self-compassion?*

CONCLUSION

You have reached the end of this volume, but the journey toward a more organized and peaceful life is just beginning. Throughout these pages, we've explored a new approach, one that rejects rigid rules and embraces the unique wiring of the ADHD brain. We've learned that organization is not about achieving a flawless, static state, but about building flexible, compassionate systems that support your life as it actually is.

You've built a new mental toolkit. You now have a framework for shifting your mindset from overwhelm to empowerment. You have strategies for creating routines that work with your energy, not against it. You've learned how to turn tedious chores into manageable games and how to use technology as an ally. Most importantly, you've learned the art of self-compassion and the power of the rebound—the most critical skills for long-term consistency.

The goal is not to eliminate all chaos, but to manage it in a way that frees up your mental energy for the things that truly matter: your passions, your relationships, and your well-being. Your organized future is not a destination; it's a continuous practice of showing up for yourself, one small, imperfect step at a time. Embrace your neurodiversity as the superpower it is, and continue to build a life that is not just organized, but also authentic and joyful.

The Mindset Shift: From Overwhelm to Empowerment

The most significant change you've made is not in your home, but in your mind. Before this journey, you may have viewed your struggles with organization as a personal failure. Now, you understand them as a challenge that can be overcome with the right tools and a compassionate perspective. This is a fundamental shift from a mindset of **overwhelm** to one of **empowerment**.

Embrace "Functional Chaos"

The idea of a perfectly tidy, minimalist home is often an impossible and ultimately demotivating goal. Instead of striving for perfection, embrace the concept of **"functional chaos."** This means accepting that your life will not always be Pinterest-perfect, but that the systems you have in place will allow you to quickly find what you need and reset your space when necessary. Your home doesn't need to be tidy 24/7; it just needs to be functional. A system of "chaos containers", a designated basket for miscellaneous items on a countertop, for example can contain the mess until you have the energy to deal with it. This is not laziness; it's a strategic, low-friction solution to the reality of daily life.

The "Good Enough" Principle

For the ADHD brain, the pursuit of perfection can be a powerful inhibitor. The thought, "If I can't do this perfectly, I shouldn't do it at all," is a common trigger for **task paralysis**. You've now learned to counter this with the **"Good Enough" principle**. This is the understanding that a 10-minute tidy is far better than a two-hour tidy that never happens. It's about accepting that progress, not perfection, is the goal. When you find yourself getting stuck, ask yourself, "What is the smallest, easiest version of this task that I can do right now?" The answer is always "good enough."

Externalizing the Brain: The Physical-Digital Hybrid

This book has shown you how to use external tools to compensate for internal challenges. You've learned to build a **physical-digital hybrid system** that works for you. This system combines the tactile satisfaction of physical tools with the reliability of digital ones.

Tips for your hybrid system:

- **The Physical "Launchpad":** Create a dedicated physical space near your front door for keys, wallet, and phone. This simple, visible location externalizes the task of remembering where you put your most important items.

- **The Digital "Brain Dump":** Use a single notes or to-do list app as a catch-all for every thought, task, and idea that pops into your head. Don't worry about organizing it immediately. Just get it out of your head and into a trusted system.
- **The "Sensory" System:** Use visual timers for time-blocking, color-coding for calendars, and tactile cues like a small, physical "done" box to make your progress tangible and perceivable.

Advanced Strategies for Sustained Momentum

As you continue your journey, you can build on the foundational principles from this book with more advanced strategies. These are tools for sustained momentum, designed to keep your systems running smoothly over the long haul.

Tip: The Weekly Reset

A **"Weekly Reset"** is a dedicated 30-60 minute ritual at the end of each week (e.g., Sunday night) to prepare for the week ahead. This ritual is a strategic investment in your future peace of mind.

How to do a Weekly Reset:

1. **Clear the Clutter:** Spend 15 minutes clearing the main chaos hotspots: your kitchen counter, your desk, and your entryway. This doesn't have to be a deep clean, just a quick tidy to create a blank slate.

2. **Plan Your Week:** Review your calendar and your digital to-do list. Block out time for important appointments, but also block out time for your "focus sprints" and "10-minute tidies."

3. **Future-Self Prep:** Do one small thing that will make your future week easier. Lay out your clothes for Monday, pack your gym bag, or prepare your lunch. This simple act of foresight is an act of self-compassion.

This weekly ritual provides a powerful sense of closure for the past week and a feeling of control for the week to come, which can significantly reduce Sunday-night anxiety.

Tip: The "Future You" Method

The "Future You" method is about recognizing that your current self is in a position to make your future self's life easier. It's a powerful framework for building habits. Every time you finish a task, ask yourself, "What is the one small thing I can do right now that will make tomorrow easier for me?"

Examples:

- **After dinner:** Instead of leaving the dishes for the morning, load them into the dishwasher. Future You will thank you for not having to face a messy kitchen first thing.
- **Before bed:** Put your phone on the charger in a different room. Future You will get a better night's sleep and won't be tempted to scroll in the morning.
- **After getting the mail:** Instead of leaving the pile on the counter, throw away the junk mail and place the important mail in a designated spot to be dealt with later.

This simple mental prompt reframes a task from a chore to an act of kindness toward yourself, which is a powerful motivator.

Tip: The "Two-Minute Rule" for Everything

You've learned to break down large tasks, but what about the small ones that pile up? The **"Two-Minute Rule"** is a simple and effective hack: If a task takes less than two minutes to complete, do it immediately. This rule is perfect for the ADHD brain's need for a quick win and a sense of accomplishment.

Examples of Two-Minute Tasks:

- Taking out the trash.
- Putting a dish in the dishwasher.
- Putting a shirt on a hanger.
- Sending a quick email.
- Taking your vitamins.

This rule prevents the small, manageable tasks from accumulating into a larger, overwhelming pile.

Tip: Habit Stacking, a Deeper Look

We've touched on **habit stacking**, but it's worth a deeper look. This is a strategy where you "stack" a new habit on top of an existing, well-established one. The cue for the new habit is the completion of the old one. This leverages the brain's existing neural pathways, making it easier to adopt a new behavior.

Tips for effective habit stacking:

- **Identify Your Existing Habits:** What are the things you do every single day without fail? (e.g., making coffee, brushing your teeth, sitting down to watch TV).
- **Choose a Simple New Habit:** Pick one small habit to stack on top. For example, "After I make my morning coffee, I will take out the trash."
- **Be Specific:** The new habit should be a clear, simple action. Avoid vague statements like "After I watch TV, I will be more productive." Instead, say, "After I watch the first 15 minutes of my show, I will get up and put away three things."

The Role of Self-Compassion in Your Daily Practice

This journey is not just about building systems; it's about building a better relationship with yourself. The **art of the rebound** is the most critical skill you have learned. It is the understanding that a moment of imperfection is not a sign of failure, but a part of a human journey.

Reframe Your Self-Talk

The voice in your head is a powerful force. You have to actively choose to replace negative, judgmental self-talk with compassionate, supportive language.

- **Instead of:** "I'm so lazy, I just couldn't get started."
- **Try:** "My energy was low today, and that's okay. I'll make a plan to start again tomorrow."
- **Instead of:** "I always mess things up."
- **Try:** "I'm still learning. My system didn't work perfectly today, so I'll adjust it for next time."

This practice of reframing is a habit in itself, and it is the foundation for all other habits. It's the difference between a slip-up that derails you for a week and one that derails you for a day.

Rest is Not Laziness

For the ADHD brain, which is often in a state of hyper-arousal, rest is not a luxury; it is a necessity. The urge to constantly "do" and the guilt that comes from "not doing" are powerful forces. You've now learned to treat rest as a strategic part of your routine. The built-in breaks in the Pomodoro Technique, the guilt-free rewards—these are all tools for giving your brain the rest and dopamine it needs to function. A tired brain is an unmotivated brain. You are not lazy for taking a break; you are being strategic.

Your Team, Your Toolkit, Your Future

You are not alone in this journey. This book has empowered you to build a team and a toolkit that supports your life.

- **Your Accountability Partner:** This person is a trusted ally who provides external motivation and helps you problem-solve.
- **Your Support System:** This is your community of loved ones who celebrate your wins and help you get back on track.
- **Your Professional Support:** If needed, an ADHD coach or a therapist can be an invaluable part of your team, providing expert guidance and a safe space to process your feelings.

These are not crutches; they are **scaffolds**. They are temporary structures that help you build something strong and stable. As your habits become more ingrained and your systems become more automated, you may find that you need less external support. The goal is to build a self-sustaining system, and your team is the launchpad for that.

The Final Word: Embracing Your Neurodiversity

This book has shown you that ADHD is not a deficit; it is a unique wiring with its own set of challenges and gifts. Your brain's ability to **hyperfocus**, your creative and divergent thinking, your unique energy are all superpowers. Your organized future is a life that is not just free from chaos, but also free to express these gifts.

By building systems that manage the day-to-day, you are freeing up your mental energy to focus on what you do best. You are building a life that is not just organized, but also authentic and joyful. The journey is not over. It is a continuous practice of showing up for yourself, one small, imperfect step at a time. Embrace your journey, celebrate your progress, and continue to build a life that is not just manageable, but extraordinary.

REFLECTION QUESTIONS

Welcome to the reflection section of this volume. You've just completed a journey through new concepts and practical tools designed to help you build a more organized and peaceful life. This is not the end of the road; in fact, it's the most important part of the process.

Information alone doesn't create change. It's only through thoughtful reflection that information becomes knowledge, and knowledge becomes action. The purpose of these questions is to help you process what you've learned and start applying these ideas to your unique life. Think of this as your personal workshop, a space to pause, consider, and begin building your own personalized toolkit.

Don't feel the need to answer every question at once. Pick the one that resonates with you most right now and give it your full attention. Grab a journal, open a note on your phone, or simply take a walk and think about it. The act of reflection is a powerful way to solidify new ideas and turn them into sustainable habits. Your organized future is waiting, and it begins with these first, intentional steps.

Book 1: The Foundations of a Flexible Routine

Reflection Question: Which of the core principles, redefining your relationship with clutter, embracing a "good enough" mindset, or the power of small wins, resonates with you the most, and why?

This question is designed to help you identify the single most impactful mindset shift from the first book. The journey toward an organized life isn't just about cleaning; it's about fundamentally changing how you think about your home and your abilities. For the ADHD brain, which can easily get bogged down in perfectionism and all-or-nothing thinking, this first step is a critical one. You must first change your internal operating system before you can effectively change your external environment.

Exercise: The Mindset Pivot

This exercise is designed to help you dive deeper into your chosen principle and make it a concrete part of your daily life.

Step 1: Identify Your Core Challenge. First, reflect on which of the three principles feels like the most powerful counter to your biggest current challenge.

- **Redefining Clutter:** Does clutter feel like a personal failing? Do you get overwhelmed by the visual noise of your home? If so, this is your principle.

- **Embracing "Good Enough":** Do you often get stuck, paralyzed by the thought that a task must be done perfectly? Do you find yourself avoiding a task entirely because you don't have the time or energy to do it "right"? If so, this is your principle.

- **The Power of Small Wins:** Does the end goal of a clean home feel so far away that it loses all motivation? Do you struggle with task initiation, feeling like your efforts won't make a difference? If so, this is your principle.

Step 2: Journal Your "Why." Now, take a few minutes to write about why this particular principle resonates so deeply with you. What specific past experiences or feelings come to mind when you think about it?

- *If you chose **Redefining Clutter**:* Write about a time a messy space caused you shame. Now, reframe that memory from the perspective of "functional chaos." What was the space trying to do for you? (e.g., "My kitchen counter was a landing zone for everything I needed, but it looked messy.") How can you create a system that meets that need without the shame?

- *If you chose **Embracing "Good Enough":** Write about a task you've been avoiding because you can't do it perfectly. Now, write down a "good enough" version of that task. (e.g., "Instead of cleaning the entire garage, I will spend 10 minutes throwing away the trash.") The goal is to get a small win, not a perfect result.

- *If you chose **The Power of Small Wins***: Write about a time you felt unmotivated. Now, identify a small win that would have given you a dopamine hit in that moment. (e.g., "I could have simply put away three items on the counter.") The goal is to train your brain to seek out these small, immediate rewards.

Step 3: Create a Mantra. Distill your reflection into a simple, memorable mantra that you can repeat to yourself when you feel overwhelmed. This mantra will be your compass, a single thought that can pull you out of a negative thought spiral.

- **For Redefining Clutter:** "My home is a tool for my life, not a showcase."
- **For Embracing "Good Enough":** "Progress, not perfection."
- **For The Power of Small Wins:** "One small thing is better than nothing."

Your ability to reframe your thinking is the ultimate skill. This exercise isn't about finding the "right" answer; it's about choosing a mindset that empowers you to take action.

Book 2: Mastering Routines and Habit Formation

Reflection Question: Which of the routines, the morning reset, the evening routine, or the weekend deep dive, do you think would have the most immediate positive impact on your life? What is one specific, tiny action you can take this week to begin implementing it?

Routines are not meant to be rigid, but to serve as supportive scaffolding for your life. For the ADHD brain, which struggles with time management and task initiation, a solid routine is a lifeline. This question pushes you to think about which part of your day is most in need of this support. By choosing one routine to focus on, you avoid the overwhelm of trying to fix everything at once. The key is to start with a single, tiny, non-negotiable action to build momentum.

Exercise: The Micro-Habit Blueprint

This exercise guides you to build a single, tiny habit that will serve as the foundation for a larger routine.

Step 1: Identify Your "Biggest Pain Point" Time. Think about your typical week. At which point do you consistently feel the most stress or chaos?

- **The Morning:** Do you feel rushed, forget things, and start the day feeling behind? If so, the **morning reset** is for you.

- **The Evening:** Does the end of your day feel like a sudden crash, with clutter accumulating and a lack of preparation for the next day? If so, the **evening routine** is for you.

- **The Weekend:** Do you feel a sense of dread about the deep cleaning that needs to be done, leading to inaction and a feeling of being overwhelmed? If so, the **weekend deep dive** is for you.

Step 2: Design Your Micro-Habit. Now, come up with one tiny, almost comically easy action that you can perform in your chosen routine. The action should take no more than two minutes.

- *For the **Morning Reset**:* Instead of, "I will make my bed and get ready," try, "I will drink a glass of water." Or, "I will put my phone on its charger." The goal is to start a chain reaction with an easy win.

- *For the **Evening Routine**:* Instead of, "I will clean the entire kitchen," try, "I will put one dish in the dishwasher." Or, "I will put my keys on the launchpad." The goal is to signal to your brain that the day is ending and the next day is being prepared for.

- *For the **Weekend Deep Dive**:* Instead of, "I will clean the whole garage," try, "I will spend five minutes throwing away the trash in the garage." Or, "I will put on a timer and a podcast and commit to working for a single song."

Step 3: Stack It. To make your micro-habit stick, you're going to use **habit stacking**. This means you'll pair your new, tiny habit with an existing habit you already perform daily.

- **Example for the Morning Reset:** "After I turn off my alarm, I will drink a glass of water."

- **Example for the Evening Routine:** "After I close my laptop, I will put my keys on the launchpad."
- **Example for the Weekend Deep Dive:** "After I make my morning coffee on Saturday, I will put on a podcast and do a single 'One-Song Tidy' in the garage."

By intentionally connecting a new, tiny action to a deeply ingrained habit, you are leveraging your brain's existing neural pathways to create a new, effortless routine.

Book 3: Decluttering and Organizing Made Easy

Reflection Question: Which of the "chaos hotspots" in your own home feels the most overwhelming to you, and what is one small, manageable change you can make this week to begin a "Keep, Toss, Donate" session?

Decluttering can feel like a monumental task, especially when you have a strong emotional attachment to your belongings or when the sheer volume of items is overwhelming. This question is designed to help you identify the area that causes you the most mental distress and give you a simple, actionable strategy to begin tackling it. By starting with one small area, you can build confidence and momentum without getting stuck in overwhelm.

Exercise: The Micro-Declutter Blueprint

This exercise takes the "Keep, Toss, Donate" method and applies it in a way that is sensitive to the challenges of the ADHD brain.

Step 1: Identify Your Hottest Hotspot. Walk through your home and identify the single space that makes you feel the most defeated. This is your "chaos hotspot."

- Is it the **kitchen counter** where mail, keys, and random items accumulate?
- Is it your **desk** where papers and half-finished projects pile up?
- Is it the **chair in your bedroom** that has become a clothes rack?
- Is it a **drawer** you haven't opened in years?

Step 2: Introduce a "Chaos Container." The first step is not to get rid of anything. The first step is to contain the chaos. Find a simple, non-judgmental container—a basket, a box, a bag—and place it next to your hotspot. The container's purpose is to act as a temporary holding zone. All the items that don't belong in that space will be placed in the container. This simple act of containment provides immediate visual relief and a sense of control.

Step 3: Schedule a "One-Song Session." Now, schedule a single, low-pressure session this week to deal with the contents of that container. Put on one of your favorite high-dopamine songs and commit to working only for the duration of that song.

- **Keep:** For each item, ask yourself: "Does this item serve a clear purpose, and do I have a home for it?" If yes, find its home immediately.
- **Toss:** If the item is clearly trash, toss it.
- **Donate:** If the item is something you no longer need but is in good condition, place it in a designated donation box.

Tip: The key is to be ruthless in your decisions. If an item doesn't have a clear home, or if you can't remember the last time you used it, it's likely a candidate for the Toss or Donate pile. The goal of this session is not to get rid of everything, but to make a few decisions that will get the ball rolling.

Step 4: Celebrate! After the song ends, stop immediately, regardless of whether you're finished. You've completed your task. Take a moment to look at your now-clearer hotspot and give yourself a verbal acknowledgment. "I did it!" or "Boom! I've started the process." This small act of celebration reinforces the positive behavior and gives you the dopamine hit you need to feel motivated to do it again.

Book 4: The Cleaning Toolkit and Time Management

Reflection Question: What is one time-blocking or gamification technique you could try this week to make a specific chore more manageable?

For the ADHD brain, a chore is often a tedious, unrewarding task that is easy to put off. The long-term reward of a clean home is often not enough to motivate action in the moment. This question asks you to think strategically about how to make a chore more appealing by either making it a time-bound challenge or a rewarding game. This is a direct application of the principle of **dopamine stacking**, where you pair a low-interest task with a high-interest one.

Exercise: The Chore-Game Blueprint

This exercise helps you turn a chore you dread into a game you can win.

Step 1: Identify Your Most Dreaded Chore. Think about the one recurring chore that you consistently avoid. This is your target.

- Is it **doing the dishes**?
- Is it **taking out the trash**?
- Is it **folding laundry**?
- Is it **wiping down the bathroom counter**?

Step 2: Choose Your Game. Now, choose a game that will make the chore feel more engaging.

- **The "Beat the Clock" Game:** Set a timer for 10 minutes and challenge yourself to see how much of the chore you can get done in that time. The ticking clock provides a sense of urgency and a finish line, which is highly motivating.

- **The "One-Song Tidy" Game:** Put on a favorite song and commit to working only for the duration of that song. The music provides a rhythmic anchor for your focus, and the song's end provides a clear finish line.

- **The "Power Hour" Game:** For a larger task, break it into 15-minute intervals. Do a 15-minute sprint, take a 5-minute break, do another 15-minute sprint, and so on. This uses the principles of the Pomodoro Technique to make a large task feel manageable.

- **The "Dopamine Stacking" Game:** Pair the chore with something you genuinely enjoy. For example, listen to a specific podcast or audiobook *only while* you are doing that chore. This makes the chore the price of admission for a high-dopamine activity.

Step 3: Prep Your "Game" Station. Before you start the game, make sure your "game station" is ready.

- *For a time-based game:* Have your timer or phone ready.
- *For a music-based game:* Have your playlist or headphones ready.
- *For a dopamine-stacking game:* Have your podcast or audiobook ready to go.

Tip: The goal is to make the start of the game as effortless as possible. The less friction there is, the more likely you are to play.

Step 4: Celebrate! After the game is over, you win! The reward is immediate. Whether you got the chore done or just made a dent in it, the act of playing the game and the dopamine hit from your reward are the real wins.

Book 5: Staying Consistent and Bouncing Back

Reflection Question: What is one small habit you want to start building, and how will you use both a visual "chain" and a self-compassionate "rebound rule" to ensure a slip-up doesn't derail your progress?

Consistency is the ultimate goal, but for the ADHD brain, it is also the most challenging. This final question brings together the two most important concepts from this book: the proactive motivation of building a streak and the compassionate forgiveness of a slip-up. This is the art of building a sustainable, long-term practice. By combining these two principles, you are building a system that is both motivating and forgiving, which is the key to lasting change.

Exercise: The Resilience Blueprint

This exercise helps you design a habit that is built not on a foundation of perfection, but on a foundation of resilience.

Step 1: Choose a "Chainable" Habit. Pick one simple, low-effort habit that you want to perform every day.

- **Make it Simple:** The habit should take no more than 5-10 minutes. (e.g., a "10-minute tidy," a "journaling session," or a "5-minute meditation.")

- **Make it Specific:** The habit should have a clear beginning and end. (e.g., "I will put away three items from the kitchen counter," rather than "I will organize the kitchen.")
- **Make it "Stackable":** As you learned, stack this new habit on top of an existing one. (e.g., "After I brush my teeth, I will put away three items from the kitchen counter.")

Step 2: Choose Your "Chain" Tracker. Find a visual tracker that you will use every day.

- A simple wall calendar with a pen.
- A habit-tracking app on your phone.
- A small whiteboard in a central location.

The tracker's purpose is to provide a visible, tangible representation of your streak. The visual chain is a powerful, non-judgmental source of motivation.

Step 3: Design Your "Rebound Rule." Now, prepare for the inevitable slip-up. Write down your personal "Rebound Rule" and put it somewhere you can see it, such as on your tracker.

- "If I miss a day, I will not let it become two days."
- "A slip-up is a learning opportunity, not a failure."
- "No matter what happened yesterday, today is a new chance to show up for myself."

Tip: The purpose of this rule is to preemptively counter the shame and all-or-nothing thinking that often accompanies a missed day. You are preparing for imperfection.

Step 4: Put It into Practice. Now, start your chain. For every day you complete the habit, put a mark on your tracker. If you miss a day, do not beat yourself up. Acknowledge it, refer to your "Rebound Rule," and simply start again tomorrow. The true victory is not in the unbroken chain, but in your ability to get back up after you fall. This is the skill of resilience, and it is the key to a sustainable, organized life.

RESOURCE SECTION

You've now completed the five volumes of this guide and have built a comprehensive toolkit of concepts and strategies. As we know, knowledge is only the first step. The true power lies in action. This resource section is designed to be a bridge from theory to practice, providing you with a set of tangible, immediate resources to begin your journey.

Think of this as your personal command center. Whether you're looking for a quick-start guide, a flexible routine template, or a physical worksheet to get you going, you'll find it here. These resources are not rigid rules; they are scaffolding. They are designed to support you as you build your own sustainable, personalized systems.

The Quick-Start Checklist: Your First 7 Days

The first week of any new habit is the most critical. This checklist is your blueprint for getting started without feeling overwhelmed. The goal is to build momentum with low-friction, high-impact actions. Pick one item from each section and make it your mission for the day.

Day 1: Mindset and Mission

- **Acknowledge Your Wins:** Take a moment to write down one small accomplishment from the past 24 hours. It could be as simple as putting a dish in the dishwasher.

- **Embrace "Good Enough":** Identify one task you've been avoiding due to perfectionism. Write down the "good enough" version of that task.

- **Reframe Your Self-Talk:** When a negative thought about your organization arises, immediately counter it with a compassionate thought. (e.g., "I'm not lazy, my brain just needs a different approach.")

Day 2: The Physical Foundation

- **Create Your Launchpad:** Choose a specific, dedicated spot near your front door for your keys, wallet, and phone. Make it a rule to put them there every single time you come home.
- **Identify Your Chaos Hotspot:** Pick the one area in your home that causes you the most stress. This is your target for later.
- **Assemble Your Cleaning Caddy:** Fill a small caddy or basket with a few essential cleaning supplies (all-purpose cleaner, a rag, and a trash bag). Place it in a central, easy-to-access location.

Day 3: Harnessing Motivation

- **Schedule a "One-Song Tidy":** Pick one high-energy song and commit to tidying for its duration. Do not continue after the song ends.
- **Gamify a Chore:** Pick one chore you dread (e.g., doing dishes) and find a podcast or audiobook you will only listen to while doing it.
- **Choose a Visual Timer:** Use a visual timer, like a kitchen timer or a sand hourglass, for your tasks. The visual countdown provides a clear finish line that is highly motivating.

Day 4: Building a Support System

- **Find Your Accountability Partner:** Identify one person (a friend, partner, or fellow ADHD-er) you can check in with once this week.
- **Draft Your "Rebound Rule":** Write down a simple, compassionate phrase to use when you have a slip-up. (e.g., "A slip-up is not a failure. Today is a new day.")
- **Ask for Help:** Ask a partner or family member for help with one specific, low-effort task. (e.g., "Could you remind me to put the trash out on Tuesday morning?")

Day 5: Your First Routine

- **Implement a Micro-Habit:** Choose one of the routines (Morning, Evening, or Weekend) and commit to a single, tiny action for the next three days. For example, "Every evening, I will put one dish in the dishwasher."

- **Use a Habit Tracker:** Draw a simple calendar on a notepad or a whiteboard and mark an 'X' for every time you complete your micro-habit.

- **Celebrate a Win:** After you complete your micro-habit, give yourself a verbal acknowledgment or a small, tangible reward.

Printable Templates and Routines

These templates are designed to be used as a starting point. Feel free to copy them, print them, or adapt them to your own needs. The key is to make them personal, functional, and forgiving.

Sample Routine Templates

Use this template as a guide to building your own Morning, Evening, and Weekend routines. Fill in the sections with actions that make sense for your life.

Routine	Time	Habit Stack
Morning Reset	15 mins	After I **[make coffee]**, I will **[drink a glass of water]**. After I **[drink my coffee]**, I will **[do a 10-minute tidy]**. Before I **[leave the house]**, I will **[grab my keys from the launchpad]**. After I **[leave the house]**, I will **[listen to a podcast]**.

Evening Routine	30 mins	After I **[finish dinner]**, I will **[put one dish in the dishwasher]**.
		After I **[brush my teeth]**, I will **[do a 5-minute tidy in the bathroom]**.
		After I **[get into bed]**, I will **[read one page of a book]**.
Weekend Deep Dive	1-2 hours	On **[Saturday morning]**, I will **[put on a podcast]** and **[clean out one drawer]**.
		On **[Sunday afternoon]**, I will **[do a 30-minute weekly reset]** and **[plan my week]**.

The "Don't Break the Chain" Habit Tracker

This is a simple, visual template to track your progress. The goal is to build a long chain of successes. A slip-up is just a single broken link; it is not a permanent derailment. Use this tracker to visually represent your dedication to a new habit.

Habit: _____

My Rebound Rule: _____

Monthly Tracker: _____

Week 1	Mon	Tues	Wed	Thurs	Fri	Sat	Sun
	[ ]	[ ]	[ ]	[ ]	[ ]	[ ]	[ ]

Week 2	Mon	Tues	Wed	Thurs	Fri	Sat	Sun
	[ ]	[ ]	[ ]	[ ]	[ ]	[ ]	[ ]

Week 3	Mon	Tues	Wed	Thurs	Fri	Sat	Sun
	[ ]	[ ]	[ ]	[ ]	[ ]	[ ]	[ ]

Week 4	Mon	Tues	Wed	Thurs	Fri	Sat	Sun
	[ ]	[ ]	[ ]	[ ]	[ ]	[ ]	[ ]

Chaos Hotspot Worksheet

Use this worksheet to make your decluttering session more structured and less overwhelming. Focus on just one hotspot at a time. The goal is to make a few decisions, not to finish the entire space.

My Chaos Hotspot: _____

My "One-Song Tidy" Song: _____

I am a winner because I: _____

This resource section is your first, tangible step toward a more organized life. Remember that this journey is not a sprint; it's a marathon of small, intentional steps. Use these resources as a guide, but always listen to your brain. Your organized future is waiting, and it begins with these first, intentional actions.

Additional Content

This section is not required reading, but it's here to serve you if you want to go deeper. Think of it as a **toolkit of prompts and templates** you can return to whenever you feel stuck, overwhelmed, or in need of a reset. You don't need to complete every exercise. Instead, flip through, find what resonates, and let these pages meet you exactly where you are.

1. Journaling Prompts for Deeper Insight

Sometimes clarity comes not from solving problems, but from asking yourself the right questions. These prompts are designed to spark self-awareness and reveal hidden patterns.

- *What does "organized enough" look like for me—not for Pinterest, not for my neighbor, but for my real life?*
- *When I think about clutter, do I feel more shame or more relief? Why?*

- *What is one area of my home that already works for me? How can I use that success as a model elsewhere?*
- *What's the kindest story I can tell myself about why routines are hard for me?*
- *If I could wave a magic wand, which task would disappear forever—and what does that reveal about what drains me most?*

Tip: Don't rush your answers. Set a timer for 5 minutes per question and just write freely.

2. Mantra Builder Worksheet

Use this template to create your own personal mantras that interrupt shame spirals and get you back into action.

- **Trigger Thought:** "The house is such a mess, I don't even know where to start."
- **Reframed Mantra:** "One small step is enough to move me forward."

Now create three of your own:

1. Trigger: → Mantra:

2. Trigger: → Mantra:

3. Trigger: → Mantra:

Write these on sticky notes, put them on mirrors, fridge doors, or inside planners.

3. Chaos Hotspot Map

Draw a rough floor plan of your home (it doesn't need to be artistic). Mark with an ✦ or cross the areas that feel most overwhelming. Then answer:

- Which hotspot drains me the most daily?
- Which hotspot is small enough to tackle in one "one-song session"?
- Which hotspot could I outsource, delegate, or ignore for now without guilt?

This visual map helps ADHD brains see the problem spatially, making it easier to prioritize.

4. Micro-Habit Menu

Here's a ready-to-use menu of micro-habits you can pick from and stack into your routines. Cross out what doesn't fit and highlight what sparks energy.

Morning Reset Micro-Habits

- Drink one glass of water after turning off alarm.
- Put phone on charger while brushing teeth.
- Open blinds to let light in immediately.

Evening Routine Micro-Habits

- Place keys in launchpad spot after closing laptop.
- Put one dish in dishwasher before bed.
- Write tomorrow's top 1–2 tasks on a sticky note.

Weekend Reset Micro-Habits

- Throw away five items of obvious trash.
- Do a "one-song tidy" in the kitchen.
- Start laundry while making Saturday coffee.

ADHD tip: Don't try to adopt all of these. Circle ONE per category to experiment with this week.

5. Dopamine Stacking Planner

Sometimes boring chores just need a dopamine partner. Use this template to design your stack.

- **Task I Avoid:**
- **Fun Thing I Crave:**
- **Stack Plan:** "I will only [fun thing] while I [boring task]."

Examples:

- I will only listen to my favorite podcast while folding laundry.
- I will only watch my comfort TV show while decluttering papers.

- I will only drink my fancy coffee while cleaning the bathroom.

This way, the chore becomes the **price of admission** to dopamine.

6. Chain Tracker Template

Draw a simple 30-day grid on paper or use a calendar. Every day you complete your habit, mark an X, star, or symbol.

- Habit I'm tracking:
- My Rebound Rule:
- My Reward After 30 Days:

Tip: ADHD brains love visual progress. Don't underestimate how motivating a simple chain of Xs can be.

7. "Emergency Routine" Cue Card

Life gets chaotic. Instead of spiraling, create a **bare-minimum backup plan** you can pull out of your pocket. Write it on a card or your phone.

- **Morning Emergency Routine:** Brush teeth, drink water, meds.
- **Evening Emergency Routine:** Put dishes in sink, plug in phone, lights off.
- **Weekend Emergency Routine:** Clear one surface, take out trash.

These routines are not about thriving, they're about **surviving without shame.**

8. Reflection Through Movement

Reflection doesn't always need to be sitting still with a journal. ADHD brains often do their best thinking in motion. Try these alternatives:

- Record a voice memo while walking.
- Talk through prompts with a friend during a drive.
- Use sticky notes on a wall, rearranging them until patterns emerge.

The goal is to make reflection **fit your brain, not fight it.**

Closing Thoughts

This additional content is here to remind you: you don't have to rely on memory, willpower, or shame to create change. You can externalize reflection, track progress visually, and gamify the process until it feels lighter.

You now have more than questions, you have **tools.** And every tool you pick up and try is another step toward building the life you want: flexible, functional, and filled with self-compassion.

QUIZ SECTION:

YOUR ADHD ORGANIZATION AND CLEANING PROFILE

Welcome to the quiz section of this book. Think of this as a self-discovery tool rather than a test. There are no failing grades here, only insights that can help you tailor the strategies you've learned to your unique ADHD brain.

This quiz is meant to function as a mirror. Just like a mirror doesn't judge you but simply reflects back what's already there, the following questions are designed to reflect your current habits, challenges, and strengths. Too often, ADHDers have been told that they are "failing" or "falling short" when it comes to organization, consistency, or routines. That's not the case here. This space is different. Here, every answer, whether it reveals a struggle or a strength, is valuable information.

By answering honestly, you are gathering data about yourself. Think of it like running a gentle experiment. If you score lower in one area, it doesn't mean you're broken or incapable; it simply means that part of your life could benefit from a little extra support, creativity, or structure. If you score higher in another area, that's something to celebrate, it means you've already developed strategies or mindsets that work for you. This information isn't about labeling; it's about identifying patterns so you can move forward with more awareness.

How to Approach the Quiz When answering the questions, resist the temptation to choose what you think is the "right" or "ideal" answer. ADHD brains often have a strong sense of how things *should* be done, and perfectionism can sneak in and distort self-assessment. Instead, aim to answer based on what actually happens most of the time in your real life.

If, for example, a question asks about evening routines and you wish you had one but rarely follow through, the honest answer is closer to a 1 or 2. If you sometimes succeed and sometimes don't, a 3 may be more accurate. If you've managed to build consistency and it works for you most days, you might choose 4 or 5.

There's no benefit in inflating your answers to match what you think they "should" be, because the goal isn't to measure up to an outside standard. The goal is to uncover your personal baseline. From there, you can apply the tools from this book in ways that feel meaningful and sustainable for you.

The Scale: 1 to 5 Each question in the quiz will use a simple five-point scale. This scale is intentionally broad and flexible to accommodate the fluctuations that come with ADHD. No one is a perfect 5 all the time, just as no one is locked into a permanent 1. You may notice that your answers change depending on the season of life you're in, your stress levels, or even your energy on a given day. That's normal and expected.

Here's a guide to keep in mind as you rate yourself:

- **1 = Never true for me.** This statement does not reflect my experience at all.
- **2 = Rarely true.** I occasionally experience this, but it's uncommon.
- **3 = Sometimes true.** This applies to me inconsistently. It comes and goes.
- **4 = Often true.** This happens more often than not in my daily life.
- **5 = Almost always true.** This is a consistent part of my reality.

Why Honesty Matters The value of this quiz lies not in perfection, but in clarity. When you give yourself permission to be honest, without shame, without judgment, you are reclaiming agency over your story. Many people with ADHD have internalized years of criticism around organization and productivity. This exercise offers the opposite: a compassionate lens through which to see yourself.

Consider this quiz an act of self-compassion as much as self-reflection. By identifying where you struggle, you are not admitting defeat; you are opening a doorway to solutions that fit *you.* By naming your strengths, you are creating a foundation to build on.

The Big Picture When you complete this quiz, you won't just have numbers on a page. You'll have a profile that highlights your unique combination of challenges and resources. Think of it as a map. Some areas of the map may feel like rough terrain; other areas may be smooth and easy to travel. Knowing where those landscapes exist allows you to prepare better, plan routes that make sense, and pack the right tools for the journey.

Ultimately, this quiz is less about measuring who you are and more about illuminating what you need. With this knowledge, you'll be able to apply the strategies from the book with greater precision, building systems that aren't generic, but personalized, crafted for your brain, your home, and your life.

So take a deep breath, grab a pen, and dive in. Each answer is a stepping stone toward greater self-understanding and more sustainable progress.

Section One: Mindset & Foundations

This section measures your relationship with clutter, perfectionism, and the idea of progress.

1. When I see clutter in my home, I immediately feel like I've failed.

2. I often avoid starting tasks because I don't think I can do them "the right way."

3. I believe a small action (like putting away one item) is still progress toward my goals.

4. I replay past mistakes around organization in my head, which keeps me stuck.

5. I'm able to reframe clutter as a neutral signal rather than a shameful sign.

6. Perfectionism often stops me from trying at all.

7. I can acknowledge and celebrate small wins, even if the bigger project is unfinished.

8. I often compare my home or habits to other people's and feel discouraged.

9. I can remind myself that "good enough" is better than "not at all."

10. I'm beginning to shift from seeing my home as a test of character to seeing it as a tool for living.

Scoring for Section One:

- 10–20: Your mindset may be working against you more than with you. Focus on mantras, reframing, and self-compassion exercises from Book 1.

- 21–35: You are in the middle of a mindset shift. You sometimes catch yourself in shame spirals, but you are building awareness. Keep leaning on the "progress not perfection" tools.

- 36–50: You have a strong foundation of flexible thinking. You're learning to treat clutter and routines without moral judgment, which gives you more freedom to act.

Section Two: Routines & Habits

This section explores how you build and sustain daily, weekly, and seasonal rhythms.

1. My mornings often feel chaotic and rushed.

2. I have a consistent evening wind-down process that helps me transition into rest.

3. I feel like weekends are my biggest opportunity to reset, but I rarely use them well.

4. When I try to create routines, I tend to overcomplicate them.

5. I've experimented with micro-habits (very small steps that stack into larger routines).

6. I sometimes abandon routines because they feel boring or restrictive.

7. I have at least one daily anchor (like coffee, brushing teeth, or taking meds) that I build habits around.

8. I struggle with task initiation more than task completion.

9. I've used habit stacking successfully at least once in the past.

10. My routines feel flexible enough to adapt to different seasons or phases of life.

11. I can identify my "pain point times" of day and know where routines would help most.

12. I often try to change too many habits at once and end up burning out.

Scoring for Section Two:

- 12–24: Routines feel like a mystery to you. You might need to focus on just one micro-habit to build trust with yourself.

- 25–40: You're experimenting, but consistency is shaky. Try focusing on one routine anchor (like morning reset) and let it stabilize before adding others.

- 41–60: You're building strong ADHD-friendly routines. The key for you is to prevent boredom by cycling in variety and seasonal resets.

Section Three: Decluttering & Organization

This section looks at how you approach stuff—your systems, hotspots, and emotional attachments.

1. I feel overwhelmed when I think about decluttering my home.

2. I have at least one "chaos hotspot" that drains my energy daily.

3. I use the "Keep, Toss, Donate" method (or something similar) when I declutter.

4. I struggle with decision fatigue when deciding what to keep or toss.

5. I've tried using a container or basket to temporarily manage chaos.

6. Decluttering feels emotionally heavy because of guilt or attachment to items.

7. I find it easier to declutter when I set a short time limit (like one song).

8. My home has zones that actually function well and bring me calm.

9. I can celebrate progress after even a small decluttering session.

10. I sometimes avoid decluttering altogether because the job feels endless.

Scoring for Section Three:

- 10–20: Decluttering currently feels like an impossible mountain. Start with chaos containers and one-song sessions to create quick relief.
- 21–35: You've dabbled with decluttering but struggle with follow-through or guilt. Focus on neutralizing hotspots and practicing decision-making.
- 36–50: You're making progress in creating functional systems. Keep building momentum by tackling one zone at a time.

Section Four: Cleaning & Time Management

This section measures how you handle chores, cleaning, and time-based systems.

1. I often procrastinate on chores until they feel like emergencies.

2. Time-blocking or scheduling chores works well for me.

3. I've used gamification (timers, songs, challenges) to make chores easier.

4. I avoid certain cleaning tasks because they feel boring or endless.

5. I often underestimate how long cleaning will take.

6. I sometimes lose track of time while doing chores and either hyperfocus or avoid them.

7. I've tried pairing chores with enjoyable activities (like music or podcasts).

8. I feel satisfied when I complete even a partial version of a chore.

9. I know which chores are most critical to my daily functioning.

10. I sometimes overcommit to cleaning binges that leave me burned out.

11. I've experimented with "emergency routines" for chaotic days.

12. I find that visual cues (like a checklist or tracker) help me stay on task.

Scoring for Section Four:

- 12–24: Cleaning feels mostly reactive for you. Start with small gamified systems to reduce dread.
- 25–40: You've begun experimenting with tools but need more structure. Time-blocking or "beat the clock" games could help you.
- 41–60: You're integrating ADHD-friendly tools. To sustain progress, balance efficiency with rest.

Section Five: Consistency & Resilience

This section explores how you maintain progress and bounce back after setbacks.

1. I get discouraged easily when I miss a day or fall off track.

2. I've tried visual chain trackers (like calendars or apps).

3. I often give up on habits after a slip-up.

4. I can remind myself that every day is a new chance to restart.

5. I've written or used a "rebound rule" for myself.

6. I sometimes push too hard and end up burning out.

7. I can identify at least one habit I've been consistent with over time.

8. I feel motivated when I see visible progress.

9. I sometimes switch systems too often and lose consistency.

10. I've celebrated a restart after falling off track.

11. My routines feel sustainable because they are flexible.

12. I can separate my identity from my slip-ups (missing a task doesn't mean I'm a failure).

Scoring for Section Five:

- 12–24: Consistency feels fragile. Focus on resilience by building compassionate rebound rules.
- 25–40: You're practicing consistency but struggle with shame spirals. Emphasize visual tracking and self-forgiveness.
- 41–60: You're cultivating sustainable resilience. Keep embracing flexibility so you don't fall into all-or-nothing traps.

Interpreting Your Results

After you've completed all five sections, reflect on your scores. Which areas scored the lowest? That's where you may want to focus your energy first. Which areas scored the highest? These are your strengths—celebrate them, and use them as leverage in the areas where you struggle.

This quiz is not about labeling you as "good" or "bad" at organization. It's about shining a light on your unique ADHD profile so that you can work with your brain, not against it.

- High **Mindset** scores suggest you're building compassion and perspective.
- High **Routines** scores suggest you have functional anchors to build upon.
- High **Decluttering** scores suggest you're learning to manage chaos zones effectively.
- High **Cleaning & Time Management** scores suggest you're using gamification well.
- High **Consistency** scores suggest you're resilient and flexible in your progress.

If you scored low in any area, treat it not as failure, but as information. This simply shows you where more support, tools, or creative strategies could help.

Next Steps After the Quiz

1. **Choose one focus area.** Don't try to fix everything at once. ADHD brains thrive on focus.

2. **Revisit the corresponding book section.** Align your weakest area with the book that addresses it most.

3. **Pick one tool.** Don't overhaul your life—choose a single exercise (like one-song decluttering or a visual chain tracker).

4. **Track progress for two weeks.** Use a simple tracker, sticky note, or journal entry to monitor your efforts.

5. **Reflect and adjust.** If it doesn't stick, adjust the tool—not yourself.

Closing the Quiz Section

You've just completed a comprehensive self-assessment. You now have a personalized map of how ADHD interacts with your organization and cleaning systems. Remember, this quiz is not about passing or failing, it's about understanding yourself better and choosing the right tools for your brain.

Change starts with self-awareness. You've taken that step. Now, you have the power to act with intention, flexibility, and compassion.

Claim Your Free Bonus

As a thank you for reading, I've put together a powerful digital bonus pack to help you apply what you've learned — even if you only have a few minutes a day.

Inside you'll find:

✔ Quick-access emotional reset tools
✔ A printable clarity map for focus and purpose
✔ 30 powerful journaling prompts
✔ Daily progress & reflection trackers
✔ A mini affirmation deck for calm and confidence

Access below to download your full bonus pack:

https://livetolearn.lpages.co/vivian-withmore-adhd-organization-and-cleaning-5-in-1-paperback/

Or, scan the QR code

HERE'S ANOTHER BOOK BY VIVIAN WHITMORE THAT YOU MIGHT LIKE

www.ingramcontent.com/pod-product-compliance
Lightning Source LLC
Chambersburg PA
CBHW061732120626
46550CB00005B/1773